Endorsements

"A thought-provoking mix of true crime and theology. *Sleep the Sleep of the Innocent* is an account of three men on death row that considers what the Bible says about heaven and hell in context of these men's actions and final days on earth. As an attorney, this book challenged me to not only reconsider my own opinions about capital punishment, but also my own beliefs about heaven and hell. This book is a must read for young attorneys, legal professionals, and Christians of all ages."
> **Reagan Hinton, J.D., LL.M, Legal Counsel**
> **and President, Where Love Abounds**
> **Goldsboro, NC**

"*Sleep the Sleep of the Innocent* is an enjoyable read. It is also a read that will better equip people for what lies ahead on their faith journey."
> **Joshua Bender, Pastor**
> **First United Methodist Church**
> **South Amherst, Ohio**

"Dr. Slack's experience with and insights in death row prison ministry are unique in several ways. He is not only a herald of "the call" to act, which call has been biblically announced to the world, he is one who devoutly lives Christ's call with those who I call the lesser than the least. Professor Slack's keen ability to communicate his life experiences of 'the call,' and the eternal consequences of not responding to it, is frightening as well as inspiring, causing us to move out of complacency and joyfully embrace the call to which God has summoned all of us. *Sleep the Sleep of the Innocent* is a must read for all Christians from all denominations, not just those who believe their call is to prisoners. Spending time with Professor Slack through the brilliance of his communications and comparative instances of his life and lives of the condemned will be time well spent."
> **Chris Summers, Chaplain**
> **Holman Correctional Facility**
> **Atmore, Alabama**

"Dr. Slack has written a sorely needed book. Grounded in Scripture yet filled with humanity, *Sleep the Sleep of the Innocent* is a personal call to see the entirety of Jesus: though He wants us in heaven, He demands His will be done. Through powerfully-written stories about death row men, Dr. Slack masterfully documents the struggle to find your own ears to hear what He calls for you. *Sleep the Sleep of the Innocent* presents a compelling and persuasive argument that will challenge those at all points on their faith journey."
>**Michael Bednarczuk, Ph.D.**
>**Institute of Justice**
>**Arlington, Virginia**

"Thomas Jefferson cut out all the parts of the Gospels he didn't like, but Dr. Slack is calling his readers to deal with the portions of the Gospels that may not naturally sit well with them and consider the weight of the words of Jesus. *Sleep the Sleep of the Innocent* is a unique blend of haunting and hopeful. I recommend it to all who want to seriously wrestle with the often neglected words of the most influential teacher to ever live."
>**Kam Pugh, Pastor**
>**Iron City Church**
>**Birmingham, Alabama**

"*Sleep the Sleep of the Innocent* is a masterfully written, soul-stirring invitation to a deeper and more meaningful life. This is a must read for those who struggle with doing the right thing – being obedient to Christ. It is an awakening for Christians who have been lulled to sleep. *Sleep the Sleep of the Innocent* evokes the passion to do more meaningful work—the work of Christ."
>**Vernon L. Dandridge, Reverend and Founder**
>**MEGAmorphosis – Equipping Young People for Their Life's Purpose.**
>**Jackson, Mississippi**

"*Sleep the Sleep of the Innocent* is one of those rare books that challenges our comfortable theological foundations and worldview paradigms addressing the existential relationship between works, grace, salvation and hell. The book centers on the experiences of three men serving time on death row, two inmates and the author's experience through prison ministry. It provides a nuanced biblical thesis on the importance of balancing faith, love and grace with works (Jesus as Lord) according to the principles exposited in the parables of Matthew 25. Eloquently written and blending a keen journalistic style of prose with academic rigor, Dr. Slack's poignant, compelling, and encouraging work is a must, but conscious convicting, reading experience."

> **Gary Roberts, Ph.D.**
> **Regent University**
> **Virginia Beach, Virginia**

"*Sleep the Sleep of the Innocent* is a very well-written book that opens a window on the daily lives and struggles of three death row men, including the author, detailing their birth and upbringing, their family dysfunctions, the circumstances leading to crimes, and the status of their spiritual lives on death row. All three lives are analyzed on the basis of three parables found in Matthew 25 – the Parables of the Ten Virgins, Talents, and Sheep and Goats. Like Dr. Slack, I was out of my comfort zone when I visited prisoners in Cook County (IL) Jail 30 years ago. Having read Dr. Slack's book, it's time to go back to prison."

> **James A. Davids, J.D., Ph.D.**
> **Chief Counsel, Founding Freedoms Law Center**
> **Richmond, Virginia**
> **Former President, Christian Legal Society**

"Heaven is real. Hell is real. We are all destined for one or the other. Dr. Slack reminds us that we do not have to be on death row to be worried about hell and that there is hope for even those on death row. We are all on a spiritual death row until we find Christ. *Sleep the Sleep of the Innocent* is not for the faint of heart. It deals with real people including the one in the mirror. *Sleep the Sleep of the Innocent* is the rare combination of being a page turner while being thought provoking at the same time. It reminds us of who we are and what we are without Christ. Better yet it challenges us to be what we can be with Christ."

> **Kevin Cooney, Ph.D.**
> **President, Wilberforce International Institute**
> **St. Paul, Minnesota**

Sleep The Sleep of The Innocent

Three Death Row Men and Moral Lessons of Matthew 25 Parables

James D. Slack

Emeth Press
www.emethpress.com

Sleep the Sleep of the Innocent: Three Death Row Men and Moral Lessons of Matthew 25 Parables

Copyright © 2021 by James D. Slack
Printed in the United States of America on acid-free paper

All rights reserved. No part of this book may be reproduced or transmitted in any form or by any means, electronic or mechanical, including photocopying, recording, or by any information storage and retrieval system, without the written permission of the publisher, except where permitted by law. For permission to reproduce any part or form of the text, contact the publisher. www.emethpress.com.

Library of Congress Cataloging-in-Publication Data

Names: Slack, James D., 1952- author.
Title: Sleep the sleep of the innocent : three death row men and moral lessons of Matthew 25 parables / James D. Slack.
Description: Lexington : Emeth Press, [2021] | Includes bibliographical references and index. | Summary: "This book is about three death row men and their experiences in living life and trying to avoid hell. Each death row man is viewed through a different moral lesson found in the three parables of Matthew 25. The moral lessons are: If you want to avoid hell (1) do good deeds (Parable of the 10 Virgins), (2) act righteously (Parable of the Talents), and (3) seek justice through works of compassion (Parable of the Sheep and the Goats)"-- Provided by publisher.
Identifiers: LCCN 2020051994 (print) | LCCN 2020051995 (ebook) | ISBN 9781609471712 (acid-free paper) | ISBN 9781609471729 (kindle edition)
Subjects: LCSH: Bible. Matthew, XXV--Criticism, interpretation, etc. | Future life--Christianity--Biblical teaching. | Hell--Christianity--Biblical teaching. | Death row inmates--Religious life.
Classification: LCC BS2575.52 .S575 2021 (print) | LCC BS2575.52 (ebook) | DDC 226.2/06--dc23
LC record available at https://lccn.loc.gov/2020051994
LC ebook record available at https://lccn.loc.gov/2020051995

This book is written for the glory of God.
It is dedicated to my beloved granddaughters,
Eleanor James Miller
Addison Ruth Miller
and all Bompy's future grandchildren!

And whoever welcomes a little child
like this in my name welcomes me.

—Matthew 18:5 New International Version (NIV)

Contents

Acknowledgments / xi

Prologue: Sleep the Sleep of the Innocent / xiii

Chapter 1: Hell is a Situation – Lost Ears / 1

Chapter 2: Hell is a Process – A World So Darkened / 21

Chapter 3: Hell is a State of Mind –

    On Either Side of the Barred Door / 45

Chapter 4: Hell is a Gift Still Wrapped – No Steps to the Right / 75

Chapter 5: Closer to an Innocent's Sleep – Murder's Noise / 101

References / 109

Index / 115

Acknowledgments

I am reminded of 1 Samuel 2:9, "it is not by strength that one prevails." Naturally, this includes authors. I am indebted to the following colleagues in Christian thought, literature, and practice for peer-reviewing portions of this book and/or talking with me about ideas for this book: Michael E. Bednarczuk, Ph.D., Senior Research Analyst, Institute for Justice, Arlington, Virginia; Kevin Cooney, Ph.D., President, Wilberforce International Institute, St. Paul, Minnesota; Mike Holly, M.Div., Senior Pastor, Bluff Park United Methodist Church, Hoover, Alabama; Mark LaGory, Ph.D., retired professor of Sociology and Deacon and Director of Outreach, St. Luke's Episcopal Church, Birmingham, Alabama; Amy-Jill Levine, Ph.D., University Professor of New Testament and Jewish Studies and Mary Jane Werthan Professor of Jewish Studies in the Divinity School and the College of Arts & Sciences at Vanderbilt University, Nashville, Tennessee; David MacKenzie, M.Div., Pastor, Bay Community Church, Courtenay, British Columbia, Canada; Kam Pugh, M.Div., Pastor, Iron City Church, Birmingham, Alabama; Gary Roberts, Ph.D., Professor, Robertson School of Government, Regent University, Virginia Beach, Virginia; and Chris Summers, M.A., Alabama Department of Corrections Regional and Institutional Chaplain, W.C. Holman Correctional Facility, Atmore, Alabama.

I am also grateful for the insights of several colleagues who invested time and intellect to read portions of this book from their respective faiths and/or "generalist" points of view: Joseph Candito, J.D. Attorney-at-Law, Blue Ash, Ohio; Samuel O. Chukwuemeka, Ed.D., retired college administrator, Bay Minette, Alabama; Gilbert O. Craven, M.A. Retired U.S. Navy and Civil Engineering Technician, Naval Facilities Engineering Command Atlantic, Virginia Beach, Virginia; Mary Jo DeSario, M.A., retired elementary school reading teacher, Charlottesville, Virginia; Michael Gainok, MSSE, M.Ed., mathematics teacher, Albert Powell High School, Yuba City, California; Sula Hicks, retired nurse, Hoover, Alabama; Keith Jordan, B.S., Co-Lay Leader, James River District, Virginia Conference, United Methodist Church, Suffolk, Virginia; Linda Krempin, M.A., retired elementary school English teacher, Dallas, Texas; Jen Murff, DSL, President, Millennials for Marriage and Executive Director, MENA Leadership Center, the Middle East and Richmond, Virginia; Bob Palmer, B.A., News Editor, *Jefferson Jimplecute*, Jefferson, Texas; Robert O. Schneider, Ph.D., retired professor of Political Philosophy and Public Administration, University of North Carolina – Pembroke, Pembroke, North Carolina; Lisa Sharlach, Ph.D., Associate Professor of Political Science and Director, Women's and Gender Studies, University of Alabama at Birmingham, Birmingham, Alabama.

I appreciate the Alabama Department of Corrections for allowing Chaplain Chris Summers to assist in this project. I am blessed by Pony Green permitting me to tell about her struggle after the murder of her son, Michael. I thank the editors of Emeth Press for having faith in this project. I am grateful to Tammy Peavy (Pearl, MS) and Brad Coltrane (Hoover, AL) for their skills in proof-editing.

Finally, and above all, I am blessed by my beloved family: the grandchildren; daughter and son-in-law, Sarah and Brandon; son, Sammy; and wife, Janis Dunn Slack, who for 40 years or so has tolerated me as an academic, supported me in death row ministry, and genuinely loved me as a person.

James D. Slack, Ph.D., Ph.D.
Hoover, Alabama
April 1, 2021

Prologue

Sleep the Sleep of the Innocent

About this Book

This book is about three death row men and their experiences in living life and trying to avoid hell. Each death row man is viewed through a different moral lesson found in the three parables of Matthew 25. The moral lessons are; If you want to avoid hell (1) do good deeds (Parable of the 10 Virgins), (2) act righteously (Parable of the Talents), and (3) seek justice through works of compassion (Parable of the Sheep and the Goats). These moral lessons sound simple, I know. But moral lessons always get a bit tricky when applied to the human endeavor. And there is nothing trickier than the lives of death row men. While taught by Jesus, who believed in hell, the application of the moral lessons are relevant to all readers, not just Christians.

Who are these death row men? Two were/are confined in a state prison, Holman Correctional Facility in Atmore, Alabama. Jack Trawick, on death row for 15 years, was executed. Jimmy Davis, Jr., who observed his 25th anniversary on death row a few years ago, still awaits execution. The third death row man, this author, is a free-world volunteer on death row.[1] I do not physically live there, but I reside there in substantive ways. But more importantly, I am a death row man for two reasons. First, like you, I am guilty of committing capital crimes against Christ. According to the Matthew 25 parables, disobedience is a capital crime punishable by eternal death – death to heaven is the ultimate capital punishment. Second, as per the Parable of the Sheep and the Goats, Jesus is a death row man. This fact alone requires me to be one too.

---

[1]"Free-world" means someone who lives outside of the prison. They are not convicts.

Each death row man presents an intimate, sometimes disturbing and even horrifying, story of struggle with God's moral expectation of obedience in how to live and how to avoid hell. Jack Trawick's story centers on the expectation of doing good deeds. With Jimmy Davis, Jr., the expectation is to use his talents. In my story, the expectation is to follow Jesus where He lives on death row.

Your life may not depend on a heaven or a hell. Your faith may dictate specifics about an afterlife, or it may leave the topic open for speculation. To you, heaven and hell may be a state of mind or an actual place: a forever reward or an eternal punishment. Heaven may be somethingness while hell may be nothingness. This book does not define heaven or hell and leaves it up to your faith or speculation. The fact remains the vast majority of Christians and Muslims in America believe in some form of heaven, as do many American Jews, Buddhists, and Hindus (Murphy, 2015). However, far fewer believe in the *hell option* of afterlife.

And I find this problematic.

About the Title

The book title comes from the William Shakespeare (2013) play about *Macbeth*. In Act 2, Scene 2, Macbeth awakes screaming from a nightmare:

> I thought I heard a voice cry, 'Sleep no more! Macbeth is murdering sleep.' Innocent sleep that soothes away all our worries. Sleep that puts each day to rest. Sleep that relieves the weary laborer and heals hurt minds. Sleep, the main course in life's feast, and the most nourishing.

Jack Trawick expressed concern about sin and its afterlife consequence. He also heard a voice crying in the night – and I will call that voice God's spirit or the Holy Spirit. From within his death row cell, Trawick confirmed the words of Shakespeare, "you have sinned if you can't *sleep the sleep of the innocent*." Like Macbeth, he suffered from the nightmare of "murdering sleep."

You may think that voice was just Jack Trawick's conscience. Perhaps. In our lives, conscience is an important ingredient. Or maybe Trawick suffered from indigestion – like the Charles Dickens (2018) character, Scrooge, thought made him see a ghost. Things like that happen, I guess. What's more, Jack Trawick was not an atheist. Like soldiers in foxholes, atheists are nonextant on death row – at least, I have never met one. But I have met many death row men, seeking faith, who are ill-prepared for this life and the afterlife. So I think it's safe to assume that voice came from God.

Whatever is believed about the afterlife – call it heaven, hell, limbo, purgatory, or a faith's fantasy – *you and I remain on death row in this lifetime*. We have committed capital crimes against Christ. All capital crimes are subject to the death penalty. ("Capital" comes from the Greek "caput.") In the case of spiritual capital crimes, the death penalty is eternal damnation, or being dead from heaven. Unlike Jack Trawick and Jimmy Davis (and perhaps Macbeth and Scrooge), we will not know in advance the exact date and hour of our execution and judgment concerning the eternal death penalty. I believe the challenge of not knowing *when* afterlife options come into play gives us ears to hear that voice crying in the night. The challenge of preparing for the moment of the Great Unknown makes us less likely to *sleep the sleep of the innocent* – or at least, not as soundly as we hope, pray, and desperately need. The capital crime against Christ invites *murder's noise* – a noise lodged deep in the soul that blocks a crystal clear view of the *spiritscape* – that also keeps us from that innocent's sleep.

Chapters in this Book

Chapter 1, *Hell is a Situation – Lost Ears*, introduces a *Jesus-Loves-Me* paradigm and a *Jesus-Means-Business* paradigm. These two paradigms explain why many people focus on heaven and forget hell. Coupled with postmodernism, the paradigms also explain why the words of Jesus are domesticated to the point that "anything goes." The chapter presents the three Mathew 25 parables and then explores the cultural and historical context of the era when Jesus professed these stories about God's expectations for avoiding hell. Rules for living become explicit and, hence, relevant to those who are not even concerned about hell. Chapter 1 concludes by outlining the application of the parables' moral lessons to the lives of the three death row men.

Chapter 2, *Hell is a Process –A World So Darkened*, presents the struggle of Jack Trawick to do good deeds. He was a sex-addicted serial killer (but knew his Shakespeare!) who cast so much pain and agony onto his victims. As if that were not enough, Trawick inflicted incredible suffering onto his victims' loved-ones during his stay on death row. He continued their pain right up to his execution week in 2009.

Chapter 3, *Hell is a State of Mind – On Either Side of the Barred Door,* presents the struggle of Jimmy Davis, Jr. in transitioning street-talents to talents useful to God. From the first interrogation, Jimmy denied guilt and became a product of the underbelly of justice – a justice of process but not necessarily of truth. A gang leader, Davis was convicted of murdering a convenience store clerk during a robbery. (This is the most common scenario leading men to death row.) Davis' struggle centers on hate, anger, and a limited mental capacity.

Chapter 4, *Hell is a Gift Still Wrapped – No Steps to the Right,* presents the struggle of the third death row man, this author, in terms of visiting Jesus in prison. I am not a murderer or a convict, nor am I employed by the Alabama Department of Corrections. For more than 20 years, I have been a volunteer in death row ministry. I was the spiritual advisor to Jack Trawick, and I remain the spiritual advisor of Jimmy Davis, Jr. My struggle deals with comfort zone. Jesus expects me, as well as all Christians, to visit Him obediently wherever He works. This includes death row. My chapter is about my struggle to follow obediently and the capital crimes I commit against Christ in failing to serve the least of His.

Chapter 5, *Closer to an Innocent's Sleep – Murder's noise,* returns to the issues of postmodernism and domestication of Christ. Murder's noise blocks our ability to hear and obey God's expectations. The murder's noise comes when we commit a capital crime against God and the verdict becomes eternal damnation and, thereby, dead to heaven. The chapter compares findings of the three death row men and their respective struggles in obedience. It concludes with hope for you to gain the mercy of an innocent's sleep in this lifetime. Let me repeat, *an innocent's sleep.* Given our respective walks on a death row, resulting from capital crimes against Christ, do you not have a desire to relearn how to sleep the sleep of the innocent?

Bonhoeffer's Caution

Prior to his execution, Dietrich Bonhoeffer (1995:358-367) concluded that truth comes from two intertwined sources: scripture (which is constant) and reality (which is in a state of change). He cautioned, when reality's truth does not comply with the truth of scripture, it is reality that must alter to conform with scripture. Reality's detail – its intimacy – enables an assessment of its honest and accurate alignment with scripture's moral lessons. In our case, reality's detail allows the application of the Matthew 25 parables. However, the details can be quite disturbing.

Chapters 2-4 present the detailed – intimate – stories of three death row men. The purpose of specifics is not to entertain or shock; rather, it is to give insight into the honest reality within which God's work is conducted – the intimacy within which He expects us to work for Him and comply with His expectations. Through this kind of insight, we assess the struggle in meeting God's expectations for living life and avoiding hell. For both author and reader, the choice is either to observe the conditions of God or walk away.

I chose not to walk away. I hope you choose the same.

Sources

Jack Trawick and Jimmy Davis, Jr. gave permission to tell their stories. I knew Jack Trawick from about 2005 to his execution in 2009. I have known Jimmy Davis from around 2005 to the present. I use sources from scripture[2], public documents, published books and articles, correspondence, and conversations. I am indebted to the work done on Jimmy Davis' early years and family life by Matthew Vernon Whalen – both through his book (Whalan, 2013) and through several phone conversations.

I have studied each man's trial and appellate records, and I have talked with their lawyers. Trawick wrote 20 letters that I kept, and most of them arrived within the last 12 months before execution. Davis has written to date over 300 letters; we have corresponded since around 2006. I spent approximately 200 hours visiting Jack, especially toward the end of his life, and over 2,000 hours visiting Jimmy during several death row ministry weekends, as well as two personal four-hour visits each month for almost a decade.

The Alabama Department of Corrections granted Chris Summers, chaplain at Holman prison, permission to contribute to the research for this book. Chaplain Summers clarified, corrected, or affirmed many issues that were either confused in my notes or cluttered in my recollection. "Anthony" is a composite of several execution junkies who took part in Jack Trawick's execution. Pony Green blessed me with permission to present, in a contemporary parable, the struggle she faced with the murder of her son, Michael.

Two Things to Remember about Heaven and Hell before You Start Reading

For those who believe in heaven and hell, particularly from the Christian faith, we face a centuries-old dilemma between the concepts of *faith-alone* and *faith-plus-deeds*. This issue is the primary reason for Martin Luther hammering his 95 theses on the door of the Wittenberg Castle church

---

[2] Unless otherwise noted, verses throughout this book come from the New International Version (NIV) of the Christian bible: Barker, Kenneth (General Editor). 1995. *The NIV Study Bible*. Grand Rapids, MI: Zondervan Publishing House.

(Simmons, 2019; Bainton, 2013). In the parable of the Pharisee and the Tax Collector (Luke 18:9-14), Jesus makes clear forgiveness of the faithful is quintessential to justification before God. Work and deeds, by themselves, do not make us worthy of heaven (Romans 3:20). It is by grace that we develop faith, and it is by faith that Christians are saved into heaven (Ephesians 2:8). Yet James 2:24 counters: "You see that a person is considered righteous by what they do and not by faith alone."

A misbelief can easily develop: God's love ensures He will overlook our wrongful actions and inactions because we somehow think all that matters to God is the spiritual (Kinnaman, 1999). *Yes, faith is key – absolutely – but you still have work to do to glorify God and thereby demonstrate faith (Hebrews 11:6).* That is, work is useless without faith that glorifies God. Being a good neighbor does not make you a good Christian. (It probably doesn't make you "good" in any faith.) Grace is something we can't earn and don't deserve, but we are called to demonstrate God-given grace as a result of experiencing it in our lives.

While scripture calls Christians by faith, it also requires obedience to His instructions.[3] Matthew 18:21-35, the parable of the Unmerciful Servant, affirms that faith and deeds are linked.[4] Jesus uses this parable to show one of His expectations for avoiding the dungeon and torture of hell, regardless of whether hell is conceived as a place or a state of nonexistence (Ehrman, 2020; Bell, 2012). There is an accountability for grace-received. Unworthy sinners (like us) who truly receive God's mercy (justification) will show this same act of mercy toward others through tangible works and deeds. If you and I do not hold to this accountability, then it demonstrates we were never truly transformed by the love and grace of God and, therefore, do not really have an intimate knowledge of God.

For Christians, the process of accepting Jesus as Savior must come part-and-parcel with acts of accepting Him as Lord (Holly, 2020). Yes, accepting Him as Savior is sought as a guarantee into heaven. However,

---

[3] After 500 years of dispute, the Lutheran and Roman Catholic churches tend to agree with the linkage between faith-unconditionally and faith-resulting-in-works. In the "Reconciliation on Justification," both concur that (1) grace gets us into heaven, but (2) to gain grace we must accept Jesus and have unconditional faith in following His commands (Radino, 2009).

[4] Here, a servant's king performs the act of forgiveness of a debt the servant cannot possibly repay. The act of forgiveness is a demonstration of grace. Yet even though the servant was afforded grace, he did not experience that grace to the point of sharing it. Because the servant did not perform the same deeds of forgiveness and mercy to another servant, the king threw him into a dungeon to be tortured until he repaid that unachievable debt.

accepting Jesus as Lord requires obedience in following His expectations. Both dimensions of Christ are required; diminishing the commitment to Him as Lord permits the fallacy that expectations are merely suggestions.

The second thing to remember is this: Although grace is essential to Christian salvation, just as some form of mercy is part of other faiths' belief in heaven, grace is not the focus of this book. While God's grace is underscored 128 times in 120 verses in the Christian bible, it is only mentioned four times in its New Testament.[5] In fact, Jesus never uses the word "grace" in any verse about heaven (Strong 2010).[6]

Postscript

Let me repeat. When it comes down to it, *we all are death row men and women* because of the capital crimes committed with respect to the expectation of obedience expressed in the Matthew 25 parables. Even if you do not believe in capital crimes against Christ, the moral lessons about doing good deeds (Parable of the Ten Virgins), acting righteously (Parable of the Talents), and engaging in justice through works of compassion (Parable of the Sheep and the Goats) arc any belief system and, hence, are relevant to all faiths and people. Even if you do not care about heaven or hell, the moral lessons about what to do in this lifetime – and the struggle to apply those moral lessons – warrant a read of this book.

---

[5] Luke 2:40, John 1:14, 1:16, and 1:17.

[6] While using the NIV version, Online Strong's Concordance gives notification when other versions have a different count. These variations are included in the totals presented throughout the book.

Chapter 1

Hell is a Situation – Lost Ears

Forgotten Hell

Jesus is concerned about hell, not just heaven. His teachings provide moral lessons on how to live life to avoid hell. A death row man ought to understand this, and a *free-world* person ought to be mindful of it, too.[1] I don't mean the "fire and brimstone" stuff about hell. Truthful sermons are important, as well as frank talks between a condemned man and his spiritual advisor. Yet there is no need to terrify people into believing in hell.[2] We need to acknowledge its existence and understand its relationship to God. Simply put: If we choose not to obey the expectations of God, we demonstrate little faith. If we have little faith, *we* choose the hell option. Because *we are all on death row*, two questions are relevant. How can we satisfy God's expectations on how to live our lives? When is it too late to learn?

This chapter concentrates on why people like to forget about hell. It then explores the cultural and historical context in which Jesus told his parables. The chapter concludes by introducing the Matthew 25 parables where Jesus lays out what must be done to avoid hell.

Lost Ears - A Contemporary Parable

This is what hell is like. A servant of the Lord made a presentation about hell to a group of free-world Christians. The servant asked, "When was the last time you heard a sermon on hell in this building?" One person thought she remembered someone preaching about hell a long time ago, but everyone else agreed they've heard not "one damn sermon" on that topic.

Then the servant linked hell with a murderer on death row. He reminded the Christians sitting before him that they, too, are on a death row. Could

---

[1] The term "free-world" refers to persons not incarcerated.

[2] Hell may be a specific place or a state of nonexistence. The point for our purpose: hell exists. See Ehrman, 2020.

the murderer go to heaven while some in the room go to hell? Would God refurbish death row with life while permitting the free-world to decay into death?

These questions infuriated many whose *spiritual* comfort zones were challenged. They stoned the servant with accusations. "You're way over the line!" "I don't need to hear this crap!" "You offend me because I'm not condemned!" One described heaven and hell as two sides of a silver dollar coin. He resolved, "We don't need to hear about the 'hell' side of that coin!" Several put their hands over their ears while others stormed out for want of hearing no more.

The servant went home and fell into a deep sleep. In a dream, he was stirred by a voice:

> Blessed are those with ears for they approach My Truth. If they don't hear My concerns about hell, how can they possibly feel My joy about heaven? Those with ears hear My voice – even in the middle of the night; especially when trying to sleep the sleep of the innocent. They understand My love. They obey My orders. Those with ears hear My every Word for they have tremendous faith. Truly I say, only those with ears will enter heaven.

The servant awoke from the dream having learned what those at the presentation could not understand. *Hell is a situation.* It entails *lost ears.*

He doesn't want to send you there, but

God created hell specifically for Satan and his angels (Revelation 20:10; Jude 1:6). However, as Gary Roberts (2015:197) reminds us:

> If God had engineered a physical and spiritual universe in which his creations were 'programmed' to preclude the possibility of choosing evil, then God would be limiting our ability to experience the key character attribute of God that provides mean and purpose, the ability to freely give or withhold the only eternal gift of value, agape love.

Agape love can never be matched or repaid. It is willingly given. It is a selfless, sacrificial love that comes to you and me even though we don't deserve it. God gives us this kind of love, and therefore, we have the option to give it freely to others. After all, free volition was the basis of Christ's decision to suffer as a human the pain of crucifixion (Philippians 2:2-8). His choice of obedience to God allowed Him to give us agape love.

Scripture consistently verifies God does not want to send us to hell. In the Old Testament, Abraham negotiates the number of righteous people needed for God to avoid judging Sodom: "Will you sweep away the righteous with the wicked?" (Genesis 18:23).[3] Eventually God agrees to save the entire population of Sodom if only a very few righteous residents can be found (Genesis 18:32). In the New Testament, Paul writes that Jesus wants all people to be saved (1Timothy 2:4). Peter reminds us that Jesus does not want anyone to perish (2 Peter 3:9). In Luke 15 – the parables of the lost sheep, the lost coin, and the lost son – Jesus demonstrates He wants us to remain with Him.

God's love for us means we end up in hell only as a *last resort*. Jesus' reluctance is similar to that of a loving parent grounding a misbehaving child who thereby misses out on the fun of a warm sunny afternoon. The child knew the consequences of wrong-doing, and it is the child, not the parent, who has chosen to do wrong. The parent loathfully shows she or he means business, and so does Jesus. Like the parent, Jesus "never sends anyone to hell against his or her will" (Roberts 2015:160). It is our actions or inactions – stemming from a lack of faith in following Him – that send us there.[4]

The bottom line is this. If we are sent to hell, it is because we did not understand His agape love. It centers on both the *personal* and the *intimate*. Personal because God's love meets each person's unique needs, despite our inability to realize it. Intimate because He expects you and me to know Him as deeply as He knows us. That means we must have faith in Him *while* we meet His expectations. He expects our faith to manifest and bloom in what we do and what we don't do.

Lost Ears are Everywhere

The forgotten hell is not unique to that small group of Christians found in the contemporary parable. A Pew survey of Americans' faith-beliefs (Murphy, 2015) shows more Muslims – 76 percent – than Christians – 67 percent – believe in hell. Among Protestant and Catholic Americans, the group with the highest level of belief in hell – 82 percent – are members of the *historically Black church*. While more Evangelicals than "main line" Protestants believe in hell, still *one in four Evangelicals does not.*

Another Pew survey (Fahmy, 2018) shows 60 percent of American Christians believe God is *not* judgmental or punitive. A Baylor Univer-

---

[3] Throughout this book, scriptures are from the New International Version NIV), *The NIV Study Bible*, Zondervan Publishing House, Grand Rapids, MI, 1995.

[4] God may give an unknown weight to dysfunctional parenting, an invincible ignorance of Him, or severe mental disabilities. *Ceteris paribus*, action and inaction make us candidates for hell.

sity study (Briggs, 2019) reports, among those American Christians who believe to some extent in hell, *less than half are absolutely certain about its existence.*

Jesus-Loves-Me versus Jesus-Means-Business

A paradigm is a framework of understanding and explanation. Readers of the Bible can discern many paradigms, but here two stand out: a paradigm of *Jesus-Loves-Me* and a paradigm of *Jesus-Means-Business.* The Jesus-Loves-Me paradigm anchors the relationship between Jesus and heaven. Through faith in His love, we are forgiven and given grace. Faith in His love is the pathway into heaven. The Jesus-Means-Business paradigm anchors the relationship between Jesus and hell. Through faith in obeying His expectations, we find work needed to avoid hell.

A problem occurs if we selectively buy into the Jesus-Loves-Me paradigm while forgetting the Jesus-Means-Business paradigm. Truth is found in Jesus' words – the **red ink**, as it was once called – to support both paradigms. Jesus truly loves us. He wants us to be in heaven. However, action is required to avoid hell.

Rootless and Homeless without Absolutes

For too many Christians, on death row and in the free-world, the Jesus-Loves-Me paradigm fits well into the spiritual comfort zone of postmodern society. Postmodernism is a philosophy that began in the 1920s. It legitimately critiques positivism – structured or "established" views of truth and reality (Woods, 1999). Its flaw, however, is the enablement of persons and social movements to "deconstruct" and "reconstruct" truth and reality to match personal needs, selfish prejudices, and hidden agendas (Trimm, 2019; Hicks, 2011). Its impact on Christianity can be seen, for instance, in the physical deconstruction of Protestant churches and their reconstruction into a single Reich Church in Nazi Germany (Steigmann-Gall. 2003). Postmodernism gave the Nazis the rationale to convince German Christians to acquiesce to the holocaust.

Dietrich Bonhoeffer (1995) witnessed the dynamics of postmodernism in Nazi Germany. In his last (unfinished) manuscript prior to being executed by the Nazis, he admits, "The truthful word is not in itself constant; it is as much alive as life itself" (p. 360). Yet he warns, "When words become *rootless and homeless*, then the word loses truth, and then indeed there must almost inevitably be lying" (p. 362, italics mine).

Postmodern rationalization took root in the U.S. in the late 1940s. William F. Buckley found colleges and universities – particularly his alma mater, Yale – becoming contaminated "with the *absolute that there are no absolutes*" (Buckley, 1986:23). Like Bonhoeffer, Buckley gave warning. If his generation did nothing to stop postmodernism as a practiced framework, "the next generation most probably will not *want* to" stop it (Buckley, 1986:103). Buckley's call went unanswered, and postmodernism became dominant by the 1970s (Hoeveler, 1996).

Christians are not immune. It is the Jesus-Loves-Me paradigm that benefits most by postmodern intrusion. The *absolute of no absolutes* dominates the hearts, minds, and, most importantly, the souls of many Christians.

Consequences

You can see the consequences at varied levels. On a simple level, look at the so-called Christian-industrial complex (Claiborne, 2016:37). Walk into any Christian gift shop and just about everything – from coffee mugs to t-shirts to books — embraces the Jesus-Loves-Me paradigm. Those t-shirts are often worn into death row by free-world volunteers, and the "love" message is the thrust of their ministry.

At a higher level, examine the web for church marketing. One church proclaims its mission as "Love God, Love One Another, Love the World." Another invites people to join as a place "to grow and share the love of Jesus Christ." Such marketing is also adapted to attract inmates to prison ministries. My point is this: Postmodernism blurs the full spectrum of God's purpose and ignores His expectations when marketing to fill free-world pews and prison chairs.

At an even higher level, the teachings of Jesus become *rootless and homeless*. Postmodernism drags down the validity – knowing what we think we are measuring or observing – of any authentic interpretation. The very nature of how we distinguish *justified belief* from simply *opinion* can be challenged by postmodernists to satisfy their spiritual comfort zones (Vanhooser, 1998:99). That is, any idea about Jesus can be deconstructed to fit into one's personal hope – and this applies to both free-world and death row Christians. As Vanhooser (1998:457) underscores, "God is a speaking God" and "most of what God does ... is accomplished by speech acts." From Bonhoeffer's (2003) *justified belief*, postmodern skepticism of God's speech-acts transforms the expectation of costly grace into the rationalization for cheap grace. Christians become spiritually lazy and filled with self-serving motive. Postmodernism gives license to biblical deconstruction of truth and the reconstruction of a damning *opinion*: Jesus' love means "anything goes" (Preach Arizona, 2008).

For instance, in John 3:17(a) Jesus proclaims, "For God did not send his Son into the world to condemn the world." Only if we deconstruct this phrase and reconstruct it to mean "the Son will *not* condemn" can rationalization occur about "anything goes." Before you know it, we are engaged in what Amy-Jill Levine (2014:300) calls a "process of domestication" of His words where we seek "more comfort with answers rather than questions."

To find comfort with answers means taking license to deconstruct many verses – including John 3:19b "men loved darkness" and John 3:20a "who does evil" – and reconstruct meaning to be compatible with the *absolute of no absolutes*. Words like "darkness" and "evil" are devalued to fit the paradigm. This grants luxury to believe you could not possibly love darkness. (In the free-world, the blame tends to go to "them." On death row, the blame tends to travel to "aggravating circumstances.") The same deconstruction permits free-world and death row Christians to avoid the confession of evil. (In the free-world, it's always the "other" person. On death row, it is usually the "partner who copped a plea.") The end game is this: Regardless of what is done in life, we can employ our last breath to rationalize wrong-doings and Jesus-Loves-Me will come to the rescue. We seek comfort without contrition. We expect reprieve without penalty. Like a well-intentioned but misguided loving parent, Jesus will release us from earth-bound time-outs just in the nick of time to enjoy the fun of the warm sunny heaven afternoon.

Standing by Itself

The most condemning effect of postmodernism on the Jesus-Loves-Me paradigm is this: Christians can accept Jesus as "Savior" while discounting Him as "Lord" (Holly, 2020). Neglecting Jesus as Lord – the Boss – eliminates the need to invest in His expectations. The Jesus-Loves-Me paradigm, when standing by itself, means expectations become suggestions and hell is forgotten.

The ramifications are dreadful. Seeking a Jesus that loves and saves us, without acknowledging He is Lord, permits the reconstruction of issues so we need not worry: hell, being left in the darkness, Jesus not knowing us, gnashing of teeth, or ending up with eternal damnation. Places of worship are reconstructed as venues of easy reading and light entertainment with uncomfortable questions replaced with "feel-good" sermons and shallow Sunday school lessons – all to fit the lowest common denominator of the spiritual comfort zone. When you add narthex giftshops, coffee carts, and, as Shane Claiborne (2016:35) describes, "cute girls, free junk food, and cheap snowboarding trips," you get a view of how postmodernism facilitates this kind of domestication through the Jesus-Loves-Me paradigm. For the man or woman on death row, the domestication of God's expectations was a major factor in travelling the path to the execution chamber. For the free-world man or woman, domestication permits the folly of a pardon at the foot of God's throne.

If we buy into the postmodern domestication process, you and I are robbed of the internal authenticity of the Christian Walk – an authenticity that only comes from rebirth and the Holy Spirit's activity in one's life. Without realizing it, our own works can easily become *concerns of process* rather than *harvests of His intent*. What Bonhoeffer realized in his day remains the same in ours: our Walk can become rootless and homeless.

The Bible Tells Me So

It's easy to understand why the Jesus-Loves-Me paradigm, standing by itself, generates Christian euphoria. One popular hymn affirms: "Jesus loves me this I know, for the Bible tells me so."[5] What children's Sunday school class does not sing this in front of the adult congregation where parents and grandparents gleefully take iphone videos. What prison Christian gathering does not have inmates and free-world volunteers tearfully sing it?

Once I sat with a pastor for Wednesday night supper. As people began to fill the fellowship hall, I asked him a simple question. How many persons in this room do you think will go to hell? The pastor could have responded like this: Jim, "I believe in hell. I just don't know who's going there. And the good news is that it's not for me to know" (Claiborne and Campolo, 2012:48). But he didn't answer that way. In whiplash manner, he jerked his head toward me and dropped his fork into the mashed potatoes on his plate. After what seemed an eternal stare, his brusque response was this: "Jesus loves everyone in this room. We are all going to heaven."

Awaiting entrance at a prison's gate near Birmingham (Alabama) to begin a Saturday faith-based retreat on a satellite death row, one clergyman added to a conversation, "There is no hell." Later that day, another comforted a group of inmates, "We're all made *Imago Dei*. God would never hurt His image." Still another whispered to me during a break, "You know, Jim, everything the Bible says about hell does not have to be repeated."

---

[5] "Jesus Loves Me." lyrics by Anna B. Warner and music by William B. Bradbury. One story goes, when Karl Barth was asked by cheeky American theological students, after writing his Church Dogmatics, what he had learned, he replied, "Jesus loves me, this I know."

Perhaps. Yet these opinions are often repeated. David Bentley Hart (2019) takes a similar stand: God is good and, if the good God created us all, then He will certainly save us all from hell.

Where is the line between objective interpretation of scripture and postmodern rationalization? Amy-Jill Levine (2014:301) reminds us "parables will continue to be open to new understandings, but not all understandings have the same weight." She cautions, "If the interpretation requires an answer key or a decoder ring, then we are not hearing it as those who first heard it did." In the words of Bonhoeffer and Buckley, postmodernism commences when we permit the Word to become *rootless* and *homeless* with *absolutely no absolutes*. At that point, *we have lost ears.*

If the pastor at the Wednesday night supper and the clergy at the death row retreat are on target about the certainty of heaven because He loves us, why then must we have that meeting at the Foot of the Throne? What should be said to the condemned man or woman on death row or in the free-world? Will it just be a time for finalizing confessions, issuing apologies, and room selection prior to automatic admission? Will it be a cheesy meet-and-greet in the lobby before our rooms are actually ready? Standing by itself, the Jesus-Loves-Me paradigm suggests little more.

The Hell Side of That Coin

The second paradigm, Jesus-Means-Business, is one of Jesus warning about hell. Here He truly *is* Lord and full of expectations. He is the Boss who assigns us work. But the good news is this: work done in obedience to His expectations will gain entry into heaven – if our hearts are authentically faithful. If we do not meet the expectations, the Boss will personally take care of business. Go ahead, don't follow the instructions; He will send you (or me) to hell.

The Jesus-Means-Business paradigm calls into question everything we do in this lifetime. Will things really be okay for me at the Foot of the Throne? Will admission to heaven still be based on the "anything goes" pass I've jammed into my front pocket a long time ago? Will Jesus defend me? Or, like a good parent, will He punish me *because* of His love? Will I be sent to an eternal time-out corner while He walks by as if He doesn't know me? These questions should give everyone pause.

Again, please understand, both paradigms are faithful to scripture. Together, both paradigms present a full-dimensional Jesus. The problem is too many deconstruct the red ink to the point where the Jesus-Means-Business paradigm is reconstructed to imply Jesus-means-not-a-whole-lot. We selectively follow some "suggestions" – the easier, more comfortable ones – and forget to obey all His expectations to get past the Foot of the Throne.

And is that hymn correct? You remember, *Jesus Loves Me*. Does the Christian Bible really tell us so? Absolutely! Jesus speaks of love 26 times (Strong, 2010).[6] However, in 22 verses Jesus is *not* speaking about His love for *you and me*. He speaks about loving each other, misplaced love invested in worldly things, and the commandment to love God. The four verses that verify "Jesus loves me, this I know" are only found in the Gospel of John.[7]

Wait a minute!

The Jesus-Loves-Me paradigm is based on just four verses? Surely there must be other verses assuring His love for us – and that His love eliminates the hell option.

The answer is no (Strong, 2010).

In the single verse that Jesus links going to heaven with His love for a particular man (a rich man), expectations arise. "Jesus looked at him and loved him. 'One thing you lack,' he said. 'Go, sell everything you have and give to the poor, and you will have treasure in heaven'" (Mark 10:21a). Even verses about Jesus' forgiveness do not indicate that forgiveness gives a lock on heaven.[8] While God's grace is underscored 128 times in 120 verses, it is only mentioned *four* times in the New Testament.[9] Yet Jesus never uses the word "grace" in any verse about heaven (Strong 2010).

On the other hand, the Jesus-Means-Business paradigm is supported by 36 warnings directly from Jesus (Strong, 2010).[10] If Jesus speaks more times about the possibility of hell than about His love leading to

---

[6] Matthew 5:43, 44, 19:19, 22:37, 39. Mark 12:30, 31, 33. Luke 6:35, 7:47, 10:27, 20:13. John 8:42, 13:34, 35, 14:15, 21, 23, 15:9, 10, 12, 13, 17:26, 21:15, 16, 17. While using the NIV version, Online Strong's Concordance gives notification when other versions have a different count. These variations are included in the totals presented throughout the book.

[7] "As I loved you, so you must love one another." – John 13:34(b); "The one who loves me will be loved by my Father, and I too will love them" – John 14:21(b); "As the Father has loved me, so have I loved you. Now remain in my love." – John 15:9; "My command is this: love each other as I have loved you." – John 15:12

[8] Matthew 9:6, Mark 11:25, Luke 24:47

[9] Luke 2:40, John 1:14, 1:16, and 1:17.

[10] This includes 24 verses in Matthew, five in Mark, and 7 in Luke. Jesus is quite able and (reluctantly) willing to cast you and me into hell.

heaven, why do many free-world and death row Christians hide from this paradigm? Spiritual cognitive dissonance? Probably. Church marketing? That's part of it. Postmodernism? Certainly. All targeted to form a *domesticated* spiritual comfort zone.

Granted, some grew up in churches that overplayed the hell card. As Shane Claiborne and Tony Campolo (2012:50) reminisce, "The strange thing is that we didn't even hear much about Jesus; we just heard about hell." Bad "church people" is the first thing many death row inmates say about their religious experience, and their perspective is not unique. The world is filled with people hurt by opinionated congregants who have little authentic love.

So are you part of the 60 percent who believe God is *not* judgmental? Are you the one-in-four evangelical who does not believe in hell? When was the last time *you* heard a sermon on eternal damnation? How about lessons of penalty, as found in the Sermon on the Mount?

> If your right eye causes you to stumble, gouge it out and throw it away. It is better for you to lose one part of your body than for your whole body to be thrown into hell. And if your right hand causes you to stumble, cut it off and throw it away. It is better for you to lose one part of your body than for your whole body to go into hell. – Matthew 5:29-30

The Duplicity of Selective Postmodernism

Recently I taught a graduate seminar on "death policy" at a Christian university. The course focused on the *consequences* of taking life – either through abortion or execution (Slack, 2017). Student denominations were quite diverse, and therefore, you can imagine how this topic brought forth passionate discourse! Evangelicals were opposed to abortion but believed in the *lex talionis* (eye for an eye) scriptures when it came to death row inmates. Students from more theologically liberal sects supported abortion but were opposed to capital punishment. Students from Catholic and historically black traditions tended to believe both capital punishment and abortion were wrong.

After examining earthly consequences, I probed the seminar about the *eternal* consequences of taking life – by abortion, execution, or other means. Was hell in store for the condemned man who murders? What about the executioner? Was eternal damnation waiting for the mother who kills her unborn baby? What about the abortionist? What about citizens who do nothing to stop these or other kinds of life-taking?

The room suddenly quieted. I asked them why, and their explanations flowed from the Jesus-Loves-Me paradigm. In the abstract, taking human life may be evil or may be just. But an intimate experience made discussion about hell fall to the duplicity of selective postmodernism. I suspect abortion was part of the past for some in the room, and for others, it was empathy from knowing someone who had an abortion. When it came to execution, those who knew someone in prison were less inclined to support capital punishment – even among the evangelicals. Students quietly hoped there would be grace for the taking of life when it came to humans they knew. After all, Jesus loves "them," but perhaps not others. When I mentioned the expectations of God, this vibrant group of young Christian intellectuals lost ears to consider hell. Evangelicals and liberals alike suddenly desired a world with absolutely no absolutes.

But then I realized, I also have lost ears! Like my students, I can suffer from duplicity of selective postmodernism. Between 2012 and 2018, I created and edited[11] a list-serve and web-based blog for a daily devotional called *The Christian Public Servant*, which was also published annually (Cooney, et al., 2017). Each morning over 40,000 public and nonprofit professionals on six continents read it. Many devotions were written by readers, as well as the editors. I didn't realize it at the time, but not a single devotion ever connected a workplace issue with Jesus' warnings about hell. (And you'd think there would be ample experiences to link hell with *any* workplace!)

Amy-Jill Levine reminds us religion is "designed to comfort the afflicted and to afflict the comfortable." She cautions, "We do well to think of the parables of Jesus as doing the afflicting" (Levine, 2014:3). Too many Christians – in the free-world and on death row – run from the affliction of reminders that Jesus means business about hell. Like my students and me, they engage in the duplicity of selective postmodernism and have become victims to lost ears.

So what?

It is problematic for Jesus to be presented as a unidimensional character. Yet the domesticated spiritual comfort zone created by the Jesus-Loves-Me paradigm, standing by itself, is hard to beat. Everyone feels good after reading about His love, singing hymns affirming His love, and hearing sermons that ignore a darker, but real and necessary, dimension of Jesus.

---

[11] Eventually other editors joined me: Keven Cooney, Bill Dudley, Jonathan Lantz, Christopher Sean Meconnahey, Tammy L. Peavy, Stephen Pincus, and Greg Smith.

We must not question the genuine love Jesus expresses. Agape love is biblically-based, and it can be enabled through the Holy Spirit. It is His love that makes us internally spiritual and, thereby, authentic when we perform acts in His name.

However, we must also affirm the quintessentiality of the Jesus-Means-Business paradigm if the condemned – in the free-world and on death row – want to avoid hell. Affirmation is discerned in the parables of Jesus, especially those found in Matthew 25. The three parables in Matthew 25 are filled with love, but they also weigh heavily with warning – grave warning issued by Jesus. Life-shattering warning that is neither *rootless* nor *homeless* and certainly not imprisoned by *absolutely no absolutes*.

The Meaning of Parable

The word "parable" is an Anglo-French term derived from the Latin word "parabola," meaning a comparison or placing items side-by-side. The word originates from the Greek parabolē, which also means comparison. We could debate the differences between a parable and concepts like allegory and story (Macarthur, 2015). Suffice it to say, a parable is a comparative (parabolic) story with empiricism. It is familiar to the listener; although its truthfulness may remain hidden on lost ears. It should require "no external key to explain what its elements mean" (Levine, 2014:8). It offers a moral lesson that may make the listener uncomfortable (Kistemaker, 1980). Moral lessons should guide and assess what we do and what we do not do.

Overview of the Matthew 25 Parables

Matthew 25 is one of three chapters in the Gospels that is completely red ink – nothing but the words of Jesus.[12] It consists of three parables: one focusing on women, one on men, and one on people. The three parables are about the struggle to gain entrance into heaven and, more importantly, what it takes to avoid hell. Together, they present a sequential tale about meeting the expectations of God. Jesus' warnings intensify with each parable.

In the first, the parable of the Ten Virgins, the bridegroom is metaphor for Jesus. The parable ends with the bridegroom voicing rather quietly, "I don't know you." While his words might have been spoken softly, just think about the impact. How humiliating it would be if some big-shot in your line of work – someone you thought was a mentor who cared about

---

[12] The other two are Matthew 6 and John 15.

you – would say at a crowded cocktail party, "I'm sorry. Who are you? I don't know you." How much more humiliating would it be to hear Jesus say those words?

In the parable of the Talents, the master is metaphor for Jesus. Here the master grows impatient. He orders the worthless servant to be thrown out into the darkness of gnashing teeth. Despite his anger, he delegates that act to other servants.

In the third parable, the Sheep and the Goats, Jesus is furious with the inaction of those on His left. (As we will learn shortly, the "left" is metaphor for not pursuing justice through works of compassion.) He proclaims them cursed, and it is He who sends them into the eternal fires.

Hence, Jesus demonstrates rising frustration and growing reaction.[13] The escalation is matched by increasingly vivid descriptions of hell. There are things He expects, and if we choose not to do them, we show little faith in Him. If that is the case, you and I will not have a good day at the Foot of the Throne.

The Parable of the Ten Virgins

This parable is 13 verses in length. (See Chapter 2.) It is a story about ten women preparing for a great celebration: the return of the bridegroom. All the women were prepared, to one degree or another. They all had lamps, and each appeared to have oil in the lamp. They waited for his arrival, but he was late and it was getting dark. They fell asleep. As the night rolled on, oil ran out. Five women were wise enough to come well-prepared. They brought additional oil. Five women were foolish enough to be less prepared. They did not bring extra oil. The Wise refused to give oil to the Foolish who, as a result, must go elsewhere to purchase more oil. In the meantime, the bridegroom arrived. The Wise were rewarded for their good deed. They escorted him into the banquet hall. Later the Foolish arrived but the door was locked. They begged the bridegroom to let them in; after all, they did a good deed by waiting on him into the night. However, he replied, "I don't know you."

True to parabola form, there is symmetrical comparison. The Foolish are compared to the Wise – in preparation, as they wait for the bridegroom, and when they are on the opposite sides of the locked door.

---

[13] The escalation is also informed by the chronology. Jesus is getting increasingly blunt as He nears His final days on earth. Of the six times that Matthew's gospel mentions the "gnashing of teeth," half are in the last week of Jesus' life.

Moral lesson: It is not just the unprepared who Jesus will not know. It is also the *less* prepared. Be well-prepared to do good deeds.

The Parable of the Talents

This parable includes 17 verses. (See Chapter 3.) It presents a story of a master leaving on a journey. He entrusted his wealth (talents) to three servants. With varying amount of talents, two servants found opportunities to invest what the master gave them – and did so in ways that prospered him. Investment in opportunities is risky business, but the two servants seemed to know the master and appeared confident in their decisions. The third servant was lazy and afraid of risk-taking. He buried the talent given to him. That servant returned no more than what the master gave him.

The master was pleased with the first two servants as they acted righteously. The master promised rewards would come to them. The master was upset with the third servant. He accused the "wicked, lazy" one of not seeking opportunities to invest the talent. (As we will learn, he failed to act righteously.) The master instructed other servants to throw the wicked, lazy servant "into the darkness, where there would be weeping and gnashing of teeth."

This parable also follows the pattern of symmetrical comparison. It contrasts the act of the energetic servants with the act of the lazy one. The comparison of reward and punishment is also apparent.

Moral Lesson: It takes more than just talent to get into heaven. To avoid hell, we must seek every opportunity to invest God-given talents – even those talents that lie dormant – because this is the way we act righteously and become good and faithful servants.

The Parable of the Sheep and the Goats

This parable has 16 verses (see Chapter 4) and is distinctively different from the other two parables. Here the casting changes. In the Ten Virgins and the Talents, Jesus utilizes star characters – respectively, the returning bridegroom and the master on a journey. In the Sheep and the Goats, Jesus is the star. No pretense of metaphor. Jesus talks about himself and what he will do.[14]

In the Sheep and the Goats, the room is filled with Christians and so-called Christians. How do we know this? Everyone calls Jesus "Lord." J. Gresham Machen (2013) underscores that the Greek phrase used by Jesus in Matthew 25:40 for "brothers and sisters" – *anthropon* – actually references *believers* in Christ.[15]

Jesus commended the ones on the right – the sheep – for doing what He expected. As we will learn shortly, these are the people who sought justice through works of compassion. And compassion requires authenticity in one's heart and intimacy in the work of visiting and caring for Jesus – casting away all superficiality. They didn't just send a postcard to Jesus when He was ill or a birthday card when He was imprisoned. They *knew* Jesus intimately, and He knew them because of their authenticity. They did not "electronically" write a check to a homeless mission while ignoring the *immediate* homeless Jesus begging on the side of the first century interstate entrance ramp. The "sheep" were shocked that Jesus knows exactly what each did: treated the least of His like they would have treated Jesus. Whether or not fully realizing it, they did so because the least of His *is* Jesus, and through works of compassion, justice reigned. Jesus rewarded them with the kingdom of heaven.

---

[14] In addition, this parable is part of the Olivet Discourse found only in the Synoptic Gospels (Matthew 24, 25, Mark 13, Luke 21). The Olivet Discourse is about the apocalypse. The wording is apocalyptic – focusing on pending suffering and catastrophe for a much larger group of Christians than just a handful of virgins or one lazy servant (Smith, 2013). Failure to live up to Jesus' expectations is an expression of evil. It's not just sinful acts that Jesus hates. He despises the omission of deeds. In this parable, Jesus proclaims what He will do to those who omit deeds.

[15] However, let's still suppose these were nonbelievers who called Him "Lord" in a last ditch effort to exchange the ticket to hell. Or perhaps each had a Jesus-Loves-Me pass stuffed down their respective front pockets. In any case, remember to whom Jesus was professing. His audience was Jewish, not atheist. They worshiped the God of Abraham. Curiosity – or prevenient grace (Shelton, 2014) – may have brought them to His "classroom," but it was the Good Professor who kept them seated. Jesus knew His audience and structured the parable accordingly. His words may have been extemporaneous, but they were also intentional. The parable was for Jews who came to see Jesus and, therefore, the characters in the parable most likely matched those sitting around Jesus. Hence, if the people on the left called Him "Lord," they thought they were believers and were shocked they were not chosen to be on the right side of the room.

Not so with the those on the left. The goats must have thought they were saved Christians, probably well-intwined solely (and souly) in the "Jesus-Loves-Me" paradigm, and therefore, works of compassion were never a priority. They might have done nothing or, at best, were the ones signing cards and writing checks. They thought they knew Jesus but, as it turned out, only on a superficial basis. Whatever they did in life wasn't enough. Jesus was clearly upset with their lack of compassionate and intimate action. Rather than remaining somewhat polite in the process of "unknowing" them (the Virgins) or instructing someone else to take care of business (the Talents), Jesus personally handled this. He sent them to the "eternal fire" for "eternal punishment."

Once again in parabolic format, the comparison between the action of the sheep and the action of the goats – the right side verses the left side – is quite clear. Comparison between reward and penalty is also exact.

Moral Lesson: It takes more than words and an occasional superficial action to avoid hell. Treating the least of His *as* Jesus is certainly not an easy task. However, this is the expectation of Jesus – if we want to avoid hell.

Background to Jesus and the Matthew 25 Parables

Jesus spoke and preached at a certain time in the world. It is important to understand the Matthew 25 parables within the context of that time – if we want to map the moral lessons onto our world.

Jesus and Parable

It's obvious; Jesus was a Jew. Those listening to His parables were also Jews. Jesus fully understood the parabolic tradition in Judaism; that genre began in stories found in the Tanakh, or the Old Testament (Levine, 2014). Therefore, using parable-as-pedagogy came quite naturally to Jesus, as it did to the Jewish listeners of his day.

Jesus as the Good Professor

In the parables, Jesus is *professing*. In contrast to teaching, professing means more than restating the known. To profess requires the creation of new knowledge. In each parable, Jesus creates new knowledge – symmetrical comparisons – about life and death, self and other, right and wrong. Like a good professor, Jesus is not presenting rote lecture notes. His parables were planned but presented extemporaneously; the new knowledge was fresh and unique for each new group of "students" in every "classroom."

The Jewishness of Jesus' Culture

Jesus used the local culture to ensure His parables were understandable and meaningful. The Jewish household, for instance, typically included several generations (Kraemer, 2017). His parables had to be relevant regardless of age and experience of the listener. Further, Jesus used commonly understood metaphors. It is here we learn, oil was a Jewish euphemism for good deeds. Hiding a talent was understood as a failure to act righteously. Standing on the right, and not the left, was understood as being on the side of justice via works of compassion (Levine and Brettler, 2017).

Jewish women were taking greater responsibility in the early Christian movement. Tal Ilan (2017) makes the case that Jesus incorporates female characters into parables for this reason. In addition, food and celebration were very much part of the Jewish culture, so the incorporation of the banquet made parables familiar. The listener already knew the banquet hall was metaphor for heaven (Freidenreich, 2017).

Terrain of Jesus' Jerusalem

The local terrain explains Jesus' concept of hell. Jerusalem is surrounded by three valleys: Kidron, Tyropoean and Gehenna (Valleys of Jerusalem, 2020).[16] Children were once brought to a place in Gehenna, called Topeth, to become human sacrifices to the Ammonite god, Molech (2 Kings 23:10). During the time of Jesus, the Gehenna Valley was used as a garbage heap for Jerusalem – with a constant unbearable stench radiating from its bowels (Balfour, 2019). In that reek laid bodies of executed criminals, rotting and smoldering in the afternoon haze. Everyone who listened to Jesus' parables knew this about Gehenna.

My point is this: We can debate what hell looks like (e.g., Psalm 9:17, 2 Thessalonians 1:9, Revelation 21:8), and whether hell is a specific place or a state of nonexistence (e.g., Ehrman, 2020; Bell, 2012), but suffice it to say Jesus uses the Gehenna Valley as metaphor for hell (Balfour, 2019). To the locals listening to the parables, knowledge about Gehenna projected a visceral image of the kind of place or state-of-mind that would greet each

---

[16] The valleys acted as natural barricades against forces contemplating attacking the city.

of them if they did not comply with the expectations found in this good professor's presentation.

That visceral image is the stuff of Matthew 25.

The Holy Spirit and Jesus

The Spirit of God is mentioned 536 times in 481 verses in the Old and New Testaments (Strong, 2010). It is introduced in the second verse of the Bible: "the Spirit of God was hovering over the waters" (Genesis 1:2c). The first reference of the term "Holy Spirit" is found in Psalm 51:11, "Do not cast me from your presence or take your Holy Spirit from me." Jesus speaks of the Holy Spirit seven times in Matthew, before and after the parables of Matthew 25.[17] It's likely, therefore, Jesus' audiences of Jewish believers in the God of Abraham were familiar with the idea of the Holy Spirit. It would also be natural for Jesus to assume the symbols found in the parables of Matthew 25 – oil as good deeds, talents as acting righteously, and standing on the right side as seeking justice through works of compassion – are driven, influenced, or guided by God's Spirit, the Holy Spirit. While atheists can perform similar acts, what separates them from practicing Jews of Jesus' day – some soon to be first century practicing Christians – is a belief in the power of His Spirit.

Leon Morris and David L. Turner suggest, in reference to Matthew 25, the Holy Spirit adds a unique dynamic: a particular kind of preparation to obey the expectations of God. Morris argues a *heightened* and *constant* level of preparedness is needed. For instance, with the first parable, he cautions: "Jesus is not telling a story about something that actually happened; he is warning people of the dreadful fate of those who know that they should be watching for the coming of the Son of Man but do not do this…While there was time, they shut themselves out" (Morris, 1999: 625). Turner affirms the lack of *spiritual* preparedness causes a carelessness in life that underestimates the time we have in meeting the expectations of God. Turner counsels, "Those who do not exhibit *constant alertness* jeopardize not only their present opportunities for effective service to Jesus, but also their eternal destiny" (Turner, 2008: 597, italics mine). He argues, meeting the expectations in Matthew 25 must come through actions guided by the *Holy Spirit*. Without the Holy Spirit, the lamp lacks

---

[17] Matthew 3:16, 4:1, 10:20, 12:28, 12:31-32; 28:19. These are verses where Jesus (himself) speaks of the Holy Spirit. There are several other verses where the Holy Spirit is mentioned, but not by Jesus.

the right kind and level of oil, righteousness is done for other reasons, and compassion charters a secular path. Nothing is done to glorify God.

Capital Crimes Against Christ

A capital crime is a crime that is punishable by death. (The term "capital" is derived from the Latin "caput.") The next three chapters apply one of the three Matthew 25 parables to each death row man. Keep in mind, murder is not necessarily a capital crime.[18] Regardless of this-world crimes, the three death row men have committed *capital crimes against Christ*. In the case of Jack Trawick, his capital crime against Christ pertains to the question of good deeds (the Parable of the Ten Virgins). In the case of Jimmy Davis, Jr., his capital crime against Christ relates to the issue of investing talents (the Parable of the Talents). In the case of the third death row man, James D. Slack, my capital crime against Christ focuses on obedience in performing works of compassion for the least of His (the Parable of the Sheep and the Goats). A sentence to hell, after all, is the result of committing a capital crime against Christ. The five foolish virgins, the one lazy servant, and everyone on the left side of Jesus – all discovered too late their disobedience toward God warranted a punishment by eternal death in hell. Jesus may judge you and me leniently, but He still is judging us on the basis of capital crimes committed against Him.

As justified in the Prologue, each chapter unveils intimate details regarding capital crimes and some are graphic. However, the graphics about murder and sexual torture remain free of pornographic voyeurism. It is simply necessary to show the contemporary world in which Jesus lives and where Jesus lays out His expectations – for you and for me to follow Him. The culminating setting of each struggle is death row at Holman Correctional Facility in Atmore, Alabama.

---

[18] Within the U.S., 20 states do not have the death penalty. Throughout the world, only 12 nations consider murder a capital crime. In addition to the U.S., Singapore, Japan, United Arab Emirates, Saudi Arabia, Bahrain, Oman, Belarus, Kuwait, Qatar, Malaysia, and Taiwan.

Chapter 2

Hell is a Process – A World So Darkened

The Parable of the Ten Virgins

This chapter focuses on a death row man, Jack Trawick, and the moral lesson found in the Parable of the Ten Virgins (Illustration 2.1). There are three key verses. (1) Lord, Lord, they said, open the door for us! (2) But he replied, Truly I tell you, I don't know you. (3) Therefore keep watch, because you do not know the day or the hour.

Illustration 2.1 The Parable of the Ten Virgins
– Matthew 25:1-13

"At that time the kingdom of heaven will be like ten virgins who took their lamps and went out to meet the bridegroom. ² Five of them were foolish and five were wise. ³ The foolish ones took their lamps but did not take any oil with them. ⁴ The wise ones, however, took oil in jars along with their lamps. ⁵ The bridegroom was a long time in coming, and they all became drowsy and fell asleep.

⁶ "At midnight the cry rang out: 'Here's the bridegroom! Come out to meet him!'

⁷ "Then all the virgins woke up and trimmed their lamps. ⁸ The foolish ones said to the wise, 'Give us some of your oil; our lamps are going out.'

⁹ "'No,' they replied, 'there may not be enough for both us and you. Instead, go to those who sell oil and buy some for yourselves.'

¹⁰ "But while they were on their way to buy the oil, the bridegroom arrived. The virgins who were ready went in with him to the wedding banquet. And the door was shut.

¹¹ "Later the others also came. 'Lord, Lord,' they said, 'open the door for us!'

¹² "But he replied, 'Truly I tell you, I don't know you.'

¹³ "Therefore keep watch, because you do not know the day or the hour."

In this parable, Jesus expresses two expectations: (1) do good deeds and (2) be well-prepared to do them. It makes sense to assume God wants good deeds to be (A) constantly heightened or expanded, (B) guided by the Holy Spirit, and (C) used to glorify God (Morris, 1999; Turner, 2008). It is easy to apply these expectations and assumptions to assess the good deeds of "nice" people whose sins are considered, well, "normal." But what about those who harbor *evil* thoughts and do *evil* deeds?

The Moral Lesson

From the Parable of the Ten Virgins, the moral lesson is this: To avoid hell, be well-prepared and do good deeds.

Shunning God

Some called Jack Trawick *that monster* because of what he did to his victims and their loved-ones. However, did he meet the expectations and assumptions? Or did *that monster* shun God to the point he was no longer recognized?

As reminded in the Prologue and at the end of Chapter 1, truth about reality – its intimate detail – is required to assess the life of this death row man through the lens of the moral lesson found in the Ten Virgins parable. Its unveiling is necessary to understand the application of God's expectations in a world steeped in darkness. We must know where Christ works.

Dark Letter – A Contemporary Parable

This is what hell is like. In a letter to a beautifully voiced pop singer, a man wrote:

> Your voice could make the angels cry and the devil become pure and sweet. People like Charles Manson would melt his ice-cold heart if he would just let your music flow over him...
>
> However, I am a sexually motivated serial killer and if it were up to me – I would strip you and... Next I would slowly and methodically... just to the point of unconsciousness – let you revive and start the whole process again...You would beg for death, but I would deny you of that relief... I would – with the artistry of a skilled surgeon – ... your now useless body...

However, one night long after sending that letter to the pop star, the murderer awoke by a whisper:

> My son, I will bless you only if you use My Spirit as a wall between you

and evil desires, for it really does not matter what transpires after evil is conceived; you have already done evil. My Hand can be your lamp, and My Spirit, your oil. I will heighten and prepare you constantly to do good deeds. But if you reject My Hand and My Spirit, you shun Me. Truly I say, I will confine you to the dark without an innocent sleep.

Hell is a process in *a world so darkened* without sleep. It allows us to envision evil rather than good and act upon cruelty rather than kindness. This process can turn anyone into *that monster*.

Meet Jack Trawick

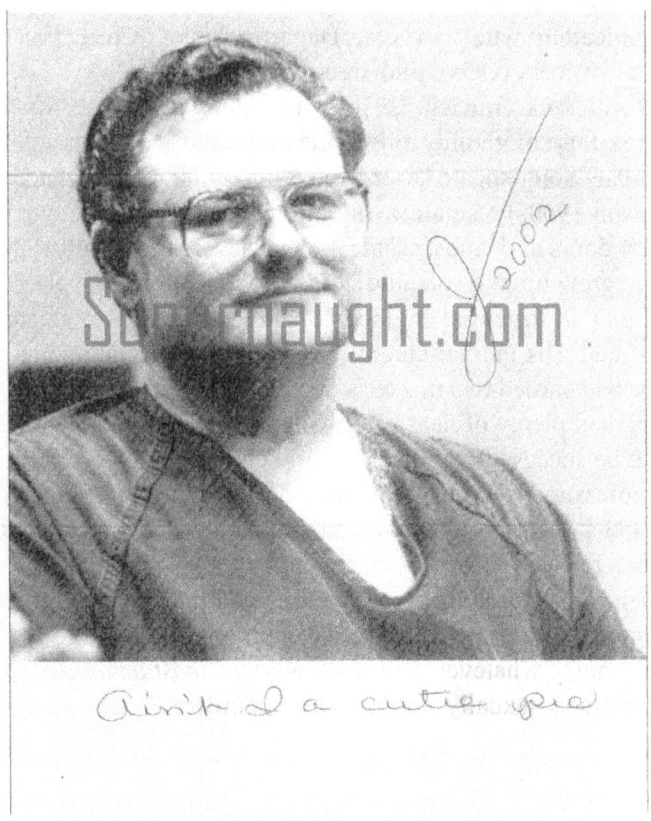

Jack Harrison Trawick was born on February 18, 1947 in Birmingham.[1] His birthplace, Alabama's largest city, is about all Jack would have in common with many of the approximately 200 other death row men in the state's Holman Prison – located west of Atmore, a town along the Florida border. Most death row men come from broken homes, impoverished neighborhoods, with only perhaps an elementary-grade education. As youngsters, they learned about beatings, sexual abuse, drug addiction, and murder. They received social demeaning from teachers and pastors, and they saw condemnation on the faces of people driving quickly by public housing while repetitively checking car door locks at stop lights in low income neighborhoods. This background converges into a myriad of challenges for death row inmates, especially in communicating with lawyers, Department of Corrections (DOC) correctional officers (COs), and free-world volunteers.

Not so with Jack Trawick. He grew up in the Mountain Brook area. By all measures, this community enjoys the highest affluence among Birmingham suburbs.[2] Sophisticated, yet Mountain Brook still had (especially in the 1950s and 1960s) a small town culture. According to Trawick, no one locked their doors and "most window shades were never pulled down."

Trawick grew up in a splendid home of God-fearing people. His father earned a Ph.D. in structural engineering and, in WWII, was an engineer on the Suez Canal. His mother taught in the international compound at Suez, Egypt. She had earned two master's degrees.[3]

Trawick had plenty of near-by cousins with whom to play. Each would grow up to be successful: a physician and chief of staff at a Florida hospital, two professors, a writer (who Jack claimed "collected diamonds as a hobby"), and a dean of a school of nursing at an Alabama university. Like his cousins, Trawick grew up intelligent and very articulate. From birth, he had every opportunity for a prosperous and meaningful life. However, there was always a *dark side*, as reflected in one comment to me: "I hope your wife is doing whatever she does – *with the least amount of suffering*." Trawick became a sexually addicted serial murderer.

---

[1] Contrary to public records, Trawick claims he was born in Suez, Egypt, where his mother and father worked during and after WWII. With the exception of a letter, no other sources verify that birthplace.

[2] Its median household income is 63% greater than the other 24 wealthiest towns in Alabama, and it ranks 89th nationally (West, 2015).

[3] Source for family background was Jack Trawick, as well as cousins who visited during the execution week.

Early Sign of Dark Deeds

There would be many signs of darkness in Trawick's life.[4] However, the earliest was sexual deviancy. He molested his little sister when both were pre-teens. A cousin confessed, "Everyone knew about *it*, but no one *did* anything about it." School officials had to know something was wrong. Trawick always walked his sister to school, but now he walked her right into her classroom – always with his arm tightly around her shoulder. He would do the same on the way home. (He said he just wanted to "test the waters," to see if anyone recognized a change in his sister's disposition.) This triggered no alert.

Strange behavior for a 10 year-old – manipulating his sister like that. Stranger still, at that age, was his keen awareness of body language. Yet nothing was done. After all, it was the late 1950s and the nightmare of familial sexual abuse remained a muffled topic. As an adult, his sister re-settled as far away as possible from Mountain Brook – in Oregon. Trawick would not hear from her until his execution day when her son sent the warden an email on behalf of his mother. She was praying for her brother's soul and asking God to be merciful.

Homicidal Impulses

It was the 1960s, and all those homes had unlocked doors and un-shaded windows. Teenager Jack Trawick was arrested for burglarizing apartments of women to whom he was sexually attracted. This required the deeds of surveilling and stalking. His sole purpose was to cut up their underwear and leave horrific messages on bedroom mirrors, written with each one's lipstick. The charge, however, was always burglary – never sex offenses – an important distinction because it denied him sexual deviance counseling while in detention. In the late 1960s, he served several short-term prison sentences for crimes ranging from impersonating a police officer to making threatening phone calls to kidnapping. In 1970, Trawick

---

[4] This included dropping out of the University of Alabama. Many drop out of college, but Trawick's reasons for doing so are troubling. "I object to filling my head full of basically useless information." A chemistry major, he felt smarter than the students and faculty. "I knew chemistry, but I also knew Shakespeare." Before his dismissal in 1967, he had a GPA of 0.03. Yet he arrogantly claimed the grades masked his approach to "genius level." Trawick was drafted and then dismissed from the military. The same arrogance played out. "Eventually me and the military agreed that the world would be a more peaceful place if we parted company…[They] were anxious to get rid of me."

was diagnosed with paranoid schizophrenia, including *homicidal impulses* (Bhamwiki, 2012).

Jack's mother tried to find help for her son. Counseling was unsuccessful. She requested the State of Alabama to chemically castrate him while incarcerated. The State refused because it did not allow chemical castration of sex offenders.[5] Besides, Trawick was never arrested for a sex crime. In 1982, she found a willing physician, and Trawick acquiesced to the procedure. However, chemical castration did not deter his desire and ability to rape women. He began the routine of trolling for women in Birmingham's Highlands area where college co-eds and professional women live.

Nothing but Deeds of Pain and Suffering

No one knew how many women Jack Trawick murdered, and the police doubted some of his stories.[6] Regardless, his dark deeds brought pain and suffering. Whether or not he acted against the woman in each story, or simply fantasized about doing so, the evil he conceived was set. That evil walled out the Holy Spirit. As he justified in one letter, "The Christian religion is founded on murder." In another, "The cornerstone of civilization is human sacrifice."

That Cutie-Pie had No Idea

Once driving in northern California, Trawick noticed a female hitchhiker. He described her as a "tasty *cutie-pie*." She was white, which was a criterion for Trawick.[7] As he told it, she wore tight blue jean cut-offs "way above the thighs," a low fitting tank-top shirt, and, he emphasized excitedly, no bra. "I was in heaven," so he "slammed the breaks."

As she approached his car so did her husband and teenage son who were standing behind a tree away from the highway. According to Jack, both males looked like they were "Bama linebackers." Rather than speeding away and looking for his next possible prey, he graciously let them in the car – "and the cutie-pie sat in front with me." With the two guys in the

---

[5] In 2019 Alabama enacted a law to provide voluntary chemical castration to sex offenders at their own expense.

[6] Trawick claimed to have murdered at least 14 women and girls. His list included: Dr. Virginia Bryant, Michelle Thomas, Susan Hall, Kim (he could not remember her last name), and others totally nameless, including a mother and her 8-year-old daughter.

[7] His bigotry would persist, even though I repeatedly reminded him my family is multi-racial.

back, Trawick wasn't going to do anything. "I just laughed and said I'd drive them *anywhere*." He looked up from our table in the visitation yard, "That cutie-pie had no idea how close she came!"

A Deliciously, Deliciously Delightful Deed

In 1972, Jack Trawick murdered his first victim, Betty Jo Richards of Quinten, Alabama. He would never be caught. As he posted on a now-defunct third-party website, "Murder is deliciously, deliciously delightful."

His modus operandi remained constant: rape, stabbing, strangulation, and a ball-peen hammer. This is a hammer typically used in metalwork. It is medium-size, not terribly heavy so sheet metal can be shaped without damage. This hammer has two heads, one flat and the other "peen" or rounded. I asked Trawick, why use such a hammer? He did not want a heavier hammer that would kill instantly, but a lighter hammer that would "reshape the head." He alternated starting with the hammer, the knife, rape, or strangulation according to the situation and the need to heighten his delight.

Now recall the contemporary parable, *Dark Letter*. This comes from Trawick's fantasy letter to Britney Spears that was posted on a website. Detailed in its uncensored version, the whole point of murder is to prolong the process of torture to match his appetite. He admired others who practiced various processes: "Most people are shocked at Charles Manson getting his followers to commit horrific crimes. From my viewpoint, I can see how easy that was – not how difficult." For Trawick, the process really was *deliciously, deliciously delightful*.

On June 17, 1992 Trawick found Frances Aileen Pruitt, allegedly a sex worker. She got into his van, and they drove to a secluded area near Birmingham's East Lake neighborhood. His hands quickly grabbed her throat. Eileen fought for her life. She shattered the passenger side window and cracked the windshield. However, Trawick was much stronger. Her last breath was taken with the back of her head jammed onto his lap while he rammed his fist down on her throat. Trawick then stabbed Aileen 53 times. Next he used the ball-peen hammer until he tired. After all that, he raped her corpse. He hid her body behind the Hill Crest Hospital.[8] Trawick once mentioned, "prostitutes were easier to get into my van and, besides, they always gave me an appetite for the *mall cutie-pies*."

---

[8] See, AL.Com, 2009; (published) "Letter by Jack Trawick," 2002.

Now Meet Stephanie Gach

Stephanie Alexis Gach was born on September 15, 1971, in Birmingham, Alabama. To say Stephanie was intelligent is an understatement; she was a member of the Central Alabama Mensa club. She was a caring, sweet person with a servant's heart. Active in church, she liked to help others, including strangers. Her mother recalls she was "enthusiastic about living her life," and that enthusiasm rubbed off on everyone who knew her. She had a sense of independence, and as her mother is fond of saying, "She marched to her own drummer" (Johnson, 2009).

Stephanie majored in psychology at the University of Montevallo, a public liberal arts institution to the south of Birmingham. The campus was reasonably close to home yet distant enough to establish her own life. Eventually Stephanie moved into an apartment in the Birmingham suburb of Irondale, about 40 miles from Montevallo.

Lucky Enough

On October 9, 1992, Stephanie Gach stopped at Irondale's Eastwood Mall. Trawick happened to be trolling there. He liked malls because he could "target a young cutie-pie" and fantasize what he would do to her if opportunity arose. It was Stephanie's misfortune that Trawick targeted her. He followed her to the mall parking lot, but it was too crowded to start his deed. Quickly going to his van, he was (as he told me) "lucky enough" to find her just pulling out. He trailed behind until she arrived at her (uncrowded) apartment parking lot.

The struggle was brief, and Trawick abducted Stephanie. Once in the van, Trawick drove her to an illegal trash dump off of Grants Mill Road in Irondale. There he committed the deed of terminating her life. He tossed the body down an embankment and drove away.

Two Years Later

It took only one day for the police to find the decaying body of Stephanie Gach. It took another two years to find and convict Jack Trawick. On October 26, 1994, Trawick was initially interrogated as a suspect in several attempted abductions of young women in the Birmingham area. At a second interrogation, the name of Stephanie Gach surfaced. Trawick denied knowing her. He was interrogated again on October 29, and this time he admitted knowing "something" about her death. On a second interrogation that day, Trawick confessed (Executed, 2009).

Before the end of 1994, Jack Trawick was tried for murdering Stephanie Gach.[9] Because he kidnapped her, an aggravating factor, he was eligible for the death penalty. At arraignment, Trawick pleaded not guilty by reason of mental disease or defect. A jury of seven men and five women found him guilty. At the sentencing phase, the jury rendered a 10-2 decision in favor of the death penalty. The judge followed the majority's recommendation. Prior to pronouncement of sentence, however, Trawick sent the judge a note: if he ever got out of prison, he would kill again. Further, if the sentence were not the death penalty, he would kill COs, inmates, and "free-world" volunteers – anyone who got in his way.

The Deeds of the New Marquis de Sade

Strange guy, Marquis de Sade – even for 18th century libertine France. He was a beloved father and a loving husband. A French nobleman, his family was devout Roman Catholic. Yet there was a darkened side.

De Sade was a writer who combined sex fantasy with mathematics to arrange characters in his novels and plays, and they engaged in perhaps the most pornographic scenes ever put to print.[10] What is more, he practiced what he fantasized. He was known throughout Europe for sex crimes against women, men, and children. So flagrant was his immorality, de Sade's name remains in our vocabulary: sadist and sadism, deriving pleasure from pain and suffering inflicted on others.

One website operator, selling memorabilia from mass murderers, dubbed Jack Trawick as the *Marquis de Sade of the 21st Century* (Bright, 2004). Third-party websites, most of which are now defunct, became the platform for this sadist awaiting execution.[11] The deeds of *that monster*

---

[9] In 1995 Trawick was convicted of the murder of Francis Aileen Pruitt while he was on death row for the murder of Stephanie Gach. Because there was no aggravating factors, like kidnapping in the case of Gach, he received a life-without-parole sentence for murdering Pruitt. He confessed to the murder of Betty Jo Richards, and there was sufficient evidence to convict, but he was not tried for that murder since he already was on death row and had another life-without-parole sentence. The State chose to accept his confession and not burden the Richards family with a trial.

[10] *Philosophy in the Boudoir* (de Sade, 1795) was banned in England for two centuries. For writing it, de Sade went to prison. Background to de Sade can be found in the "Introduction," by Francine du Plessix Gray.

[11] For instance, see NG, 2011; and Reeves, 2003. This particular website is not defunct.

centered on internet posts that inflicted further pain and suffering on his victims' loved-ones.

One post was "Jack Trawick's Philosophy 101." This included two fundamental rules: (1) never rape a woman without killing her and (2) never kill a woman without raping her. Also posted was his "murderer's manifesto," showing how to stalk a young girl, as well as explicit details on his preferred techniques of torture and death.

Trawick posted fantasy letters about his victims. In a letter to Stephanie Gach, he wrote: "Was it worth it? It was for me. I would do the whole thing again knowing death row was waiting for me. Watching you die was (is) worth it all." In another letter he mocked, "Aileen Pruitt was *only* kidnapped, raped, strangled, stabbed, beaten with a hammer, dumped on an illegal dumpsite – along an Alabama back road." Then he joked: "Sidebar: do you think the EPA will ever charge me with using an illegal roadside dump to dispose of my unwanted, broken play toy?" He even wrote a despicable letter to an 8 year-old on whom he performed his evil deeds as she was forced to stare at her mother's lifeless body.

That *dark letter* to Britney Spears concluded with a nightmarish threat. "Just think – the next time you go anywhere – I could be there waiting on you. Before you get carried away about all your security and bodyguards and blah blah blah – no security is absolute… Looking forward to our first meeting, Britney."

Trawick sent personal death row items for auction. On a website, people purchased signed letters he sent to others ($50), sketches of his nude and ravaged victims ($300 - $500), and a signed outline of his right hand ($100). The picture of Trawick in this chapter, if I had purchased it, would have cost $150. When a website operator visited during the execution week, Trawick slipped him stuff to sneak out of the prison: a Styrofoam cup from which he drank and bit down leaving deep teeth marks, a sandwich wrapper, used paper napkins, and a soda can he indented with his hand. These were auctioned starting at $15 per item. He also gave his TV to the website operator, despite it being purchased for Trawick's use by a Christian prison ministry. That small TV set went at auction for $500.

Deeds of Letters from Death Row

Jack Trawick found death row nothing like where he grew up. He remained in an 8'x5' cell 23 hours a day (24 hours per day on weekends). There were no windows, no direct heat in the winter, and no air conditioning in the summer. Each wintry night, Trawick slept wearing a sweatshirt, jacket, and knit cap. During the winter days, the chilled concrete floor meant the wardrobe stayed on. In sweltering south Alabama summer days and nights, he did what other condemned men sometimes do: jam the weekly-issued towel into his toilet and flush repeatedly. Once overflowing onto the concrete cell floor, he laid in the toilet water to cool off. Eventually some of his teeth went missing due to poor dental care. His knees and hips throbbed constantly from the concrete floors.

Cutie-Pie Pen Pals

Within this miserable environment, Trawick wrote many letters.[12] Most of his pen pals were white females between the ages of 18 and 30. They were interested in the "titillating nature of my alleged crimes."[13] He also wrote to nine teenage *cutie-pies* who wanted to "he-she with me." They would "send me pictures of themselves looking like real cutie-pies." He cautioned not to send nude photos because those would be confiscated by the DOC mail reader. So they sent photos "where their clothes are dangling, about to fall off. And they always pose real cutie-like." In return it appears the teenagers wanted "glorified descriptions of facial expressions, a sense of emotional or spiritual distress, play-by-play description of tortures."

In regard to the appropriateness of such relations with young girls, Jack had this to say:

"They are not my children. My job isn't to win the minds and hearts of cutie-pies for Christ...

Their salvation is up to them."

Between God and Me

Yet within his death row cell, and perhaps like the Marquis de Sade, Trawick was surprisingly familiar with Christianity. He consistently

---

[12] The Alabama DOC opens and reads inmate in-coming mail. It can do this because a letter sent to an inmate actually goes to the DOC as the inmate's guardian. By federal law, however, DOC cannot open out-going mail. Once the envelop is sealed and a federal stamp is affixed, it becomes property of the federal government until delivered to the person addressed on the envelop. After posting so much pain and suffering, however, Trawick's out going mail became the exception to the rule. He agreed to submit his letters unsealed to allow DOC to monitor the contents. After review, DOC would seal his envelop and mail it.

[13] Yes, Jack Trawick never directly confessed his crimes to me but did enjoy describing them.

claimed he knew Jesus as Savior and Lord and "everything's fine between God and me."

Sin and Satan

Jack Trawick knew about sin. "If an individual does something ... and cannot *sleep the sleep of the innocent*, then that person has committed a sin. If a person has to tell Jesus, 'Please look away for a minute. I must do something and I am ashamed for you to watch,' something is wrong." He underscored: "If you can't walk up to Jesus and say, 'Look what I did. Aren't you proud of me?' then you must not be able to *sleep the sleep of the innocent*."

Trawick believed his victims – not him – were guided by Satan. "I truly believe that Satan, as he tricked Eve, was not in the form of a snake. I believe he presented himself as one of the most beautiful of creatures. (His presence was pleasing to the eye.) The point? Sometimes – in fact most often – Satan sets his snare with beauty and pleasure. His option appears heavenly from the outside but is actually full of dead man's bones."[14] He then described Britney Spears as "Satan's snare" and as a "one-way ticket to nowhere."

God and Jesus

Jack had a conversational grasp on Christian scripture. "How could anyone believe God recreated the heavens and earth in 6 days" (Genesis 1), "and not be able to create a beast with 7 heads" (Revelation 13). He wrote, "I don't think God wants His children running around fearful and afraid... In fact, we are not born with a fearful spirit" (2 Timothy 1:7). However, "somewhere in the New Testament Christ is asked, 'How can we tell a difference between a false prophet – who does mighty works – and someone who is ordained and blessed by God the Father?' Jesus answered, 'Does the act .... bring glory to God or to man'" (Matthew 7:15-16)?

Trawick also pondered, "Why isn't Easter celebrated like Christmas?... It's like Easter is Christmas' ugly stepbrother... Christmas and Easter should switch priority places. Christ is born. Christ is resurrected."

His theology anchored on this: "God wants us to depend on Him. But God will never be a tyrant. He wants His children to be happy, secure, safe. But there is a catch. We are given the true privilege of free will." He surmised, "Some knuckleheads like me – use their free will in a reckless selfish manner. Hey – if you plant thistles, don't expect a rose garden."

---

[14] Referring to 2 Kings 13:21.

Anger over the Deed of His Own Execution

Perhaps expectedly, Trawick's concerns focused increasingly on his own execution. He repeatedly questioned whether the warden and the chaplain had included me on his execution witness list. "They don't realize most free-world people work and cannot on a whim jump up and take a trip on a day off and charge it to the state."

Trawick was angry with State officials. To the trial jury, the prosecutor underscored the "collateral damage" the murder did to Stephanie Gach's mother and sister. However, the impact of Trawick's execution on his own loved-ones was ignored. "Think of what the state is doing to *my* family." He regarded the death penalty as immoral until "collateral damage is taken out of the equation."

In regard to the state attorney general: "I have never seen a non-military person more interested in killing another person... I wonder if [he] realizes – one day he will stand alone before the Throne of Grace..."[15] He was also upset with the DOC: "The only thing [DOC] can do – efficiently – is kill people." As for the Governor: "I will render to Caesar what is Caesar's."[16] Then he added, "And if Caesar is wrong – he will be held responsible."[17]

With the execution drawing nearer, Jack's letters intensified with postmodern self-rationalization. He deconstructed/reconstructed capital punishment to meet his needs. "The whole death penalty-process is just a pig with lipstick on it." "The pre-mediated murder of any person is wrong... The brilliant idea is to commit a wrong to prove that another wrong was wrong... It is strictly for revenge..." "And if people actually read the Bible instead of using it as a fashion statement, they would read (see) what God says about revenge..." "If someone murdered Hitler, would it be justified morally?? Most likely because of the *good* the act brought forth... When someone murders Jack Trawick, will it be justified morally? Most likely not – because it serves no purpose except revenge with a touch of

---

[15] Throne of Grace from Hebrews 4:14-16.
[16] From Mark 12:17.
[17] From Romans 12:19.

politics…" "Show me one place in the New Testament where Jesus Christ endorses state sponsored murder?"[18]

Trawick was angriest at the execution team, including the warden and the chaplain. If the world came to an end "directly after my execution… the execution team would *not* be part of the heavenly choir… Each member had an opportunity to say, 'No – I will *not* do that'… they knew the consequences… they may, in fact, be super nice people – But they are wrong and they are lost and until they can see the light – there will be no 'rewards'."

In one of his last letters Trawick wrote, "People also need to know that ultimately everyone will stand alone before the Throne of Grace and explain their actions. If your explanations aren't in God's liking – God may say, 'Sorry, but I do not know you.'"[19]

The Day and Hour of the Bridegroom's Return

The Ten Virgins parable ends with this warning: "Keep watch, because you do not know the day or the hour" (Matthew 25:13). What if God would reveal, way in advance, the exact day and hour of your death? Would it not change you in some way? Sometimes soldiers have a feeling about such things. It is told WWI British soldiers preparing to go into no-man's land counted the minutes to their presumed deaths. But they were not certain, for prayers were still in play. Terminal patients have some sense of endtime. But they do not know exactly until the very last moment. This is why the Ten Virgins parable warns us to be prepared.

There is one place where a person knows in advance the exact day and hour of his death. That place is death row. Granted, there are years before the posting of the exact date on the condemned man's cell door. That posting in Alabama comes about 45-60 days prior to execution. And sure, there can be last minute stays, but these are atypical. And even if a delay occurs, it only leads to another designated exact day and hour for the execution.

In Alabama, as nationally, the average time on death row is 15 years. Every condemned inmate has two mandatory appeals: one at the state level and one in federal court. There are also eight nonmandatory appeals.

---

[18] I calmly responded that Jesus never challenged the death penalty for the two condemned men on either side of his cross (Luke 23:26-42), nor did He challenge his own conviction and sentence (John 19:11). Paul says he accepts his own death penalty, if it is proven he is guilty (Acts 25:11). However, because we were drawing near Trawick's execution date, I did not press the point. There was no more time for parlor games and debate.

[19] From Matthew 25:12.

Those who decline the nonmandatory appeals typically are executed within five years. Those who exercise all ten appeals may be on death row from 15 to perhaps 30 years. Time variation before execution, especially for those opting for all appeals, is a function of each case going at its own pace through the appellate process. Speed is based on the workload of the court, prosecutors, and defense lawyers.

Alabama always executes on Thursday, and the process begins at 6 p.m. The condemned inmate is strapped in the gurney, and the curtains for the three witness rooms open to view the execution chamber (Slack, 2017). The gurney is slightly tilted so the condemned can see the witnesses: to his right is the room for the victim's witnesses; center is the DOC witness room; left holds the condemned inmate's loved-ones, spiritual advisor, and two members of the press. In the chamber is the warden, the chaplain, and one CO, whose job it is to flick the condemned man's eye lashes to affirm unconsciousness after the first injection. Before that, the warden reads the death warrant and asks for last words. The warden then leaves the chamber and enters a room directly behind the condemned man's head. In this room, he administers the lethal injections, and by Alabama law, the warden is the sole executioner. The process of lethal injection typically begins around 6:10 p.m. The chaplain kneels alongside the gurney and holds in prayer the arm of the condemned. Lethal injection causes the lungs to stop working after the anesthesia takes hold, and then the heart explodes after the last injection. Death is usually no later than 6:20 p.m.

This is the process that took Jack Trawick's life on June 11, 2009, at 6:17 p.m.

Let's Back Up to Monday

Waiting for Jack Trawick in the visitation yard, I noticed the obvious. It was the first day of execution week, and no one else was in the 30'x30' glass-surrounded room.[20] Having been unshackled, Jack came through the inmate's door and, seeing me, bellowed: "I can't wait until Thursday to tell them how much their daughter loved what I did to her! She begged for more!"

---

[20] During any execution week, the condemned man has exclusive use of the room. All other visitation privileges, for death row men and inmates in general population, are temporarily suspended during the execution week. Visitation for the condemned starts around 8 a.m. and runs to about 4 p.m. Each visitor must be approved in advance by DOC. As his spiritual advisor, I was there each day for all hours; Monday and Tuesday, I was the only visitor.

Trawick was distraught because his time on death row was "shortened." His 15 years were certainly the state and national average, but Jack knew many inmates serving well beyond that amount of time. He was angry at the Gach family. Perhaps in retaliation to the pain and suffering he imposed on them, including the web postings, Stephanie's family pushed the appeals. The state attorney general and the county prosecutor, equally disturbed, had no problem convincing courts to hurry along this case.[21]

And so the last week of Jack Trawick's life started with outrage. He wanted to inflict maximum suffering through his last words. He wasn't in the mood to hear about Jesus, despite the prison chaplain having worked with him for nearly two months. As with all condemned inmates, the chaplain tried to focus Jack's attention on John 11, the death of Lazarus. He underscored verse 26, where Jesus said: "and whoever believes in me will never die. Do you believe this?" The chaplain kept reminding Jack that, as long as there is oxygen in his lungs, he has the power to invite the Holy Spirit to help him do *good deeds of healing*.

Knowing the death date for two months, Jack should have been able to process his anger toward Stephanie's family and the appellate process speed. He could not. Hence, retaliation followed anger as a primary emotion Jack embraced at the start of his execution week. He did not want to consider doing *good deeds of healing* in the remaining days of his life. This worried me because, after all, the Bridegroom was very near.

If I could only get out of here

Throughout his execution week, Trawick occasionally made racist jokes about an African-American CO, and this delighted the visiting website operator. Together they quietly mocked one visiting cousin whom they presumed was gay. When it was just him and me in the room, Trawick was prone to tell about other episodes of murder – real, fantasized, or close-calls. He asked about security on Birmingham's Highland Avenue, explaining that's where he kidnapped and murdered Dr. Virginia Bryant. A female CO walked around the glass-enclosed visitation yard to start her

---

[21] Frankly, I suspect those in the abolition movement were not saddened by the quick pace toward execution. Trawick's antics while on death row made it difficult for everyone involved with this dimension of the pro-life movement. On the afternoon of his execution, Jack would discover his lawyer filed no last-minute appeals. I was informed after the execution that many were afraid the State would make Trawick the "poster boy" for capital punishment if those appeals were submitted. This would have hurt the chances for last-minute pleas on behalf of the next condemned man or woman residing in the death cell.

shift. Knowing Trawick for years, she smiled warmly and waved at him. Waving back, he whispered to me: "If she only knew what I was thinking, she'd have no business smiling at me." At one point, Trawick gazed quietly, "If I could only get out of here today, I'd be back in business in Atmore." Yes, just ten minutes away from Holman Prison is the town of Atmore, and Jack could have continued with evil deeds – *if he could only get out of here.*

Agape Love and Good Deeds

On Tuesday, while Jack was with me in the visitation yard, COs moved his belongings from his death row cell to the *death cell* – only 15 steps from the death chamber's gurney. For the first time in 15 years, Jack slept in the solace of air conditioning and stood on the comfort of linoleum. The cell also contained a shower area, and therefore, he did not have to wait days to refresh.[22] In the death cell, Jack would be watched 24/7 by execution team members.

There would be more surprises. For Tuesday's dinner, instead of prison food, he dined on a porterhouse steak – courtesy of execution team members. Even more surprising, they brought him a three-layer chocolate cake. On Wednesday morning, they brought him a steak breakfast topped off with another three-layer chocolate cake. The execution team knew Jack was a glutton for steak and chocolate cake – desires unfulfilled for 15 years.

When Jack entered the visitation yard on Wednesday morning, he was still angry. And now he gloated, "Those schmucks are trying to make themselves feel better for killing me tomorrow." He told me about the meals, and then laughed, "That won't get them off the hook." I asked if he shared any of the cake or steaks, and he snapped, "Hell, no. They're *mine!*"

At this point, we talked on a subject covered several times – *agape love* – the love God gives freely and the kind He expects the recipient to give to others. I mentioned the execution team members risked their jobs by sneaking outside food into the prison. I inserted the possibility that maybe they surprised him with such delights for reasons other than feeling guilty about killing him. I reminded Jack what the chaplain had already told him: although he will die, the execution team will treat him (like in an emergency room) with professionalism, love, and compassion. I suggested their love and compassion included good deeds of special meals.

---

[22] On death row, each man usually has an opportunity to shower twice a week.

This conversation lasted for some time. Even after his cousins and the website operator arrived on Wednesday, Jack and I found more time to talk about agape love. Before he went back to the death cell, we prayed quietly in a corner.

Similar meals were delivered to him on Wednesday night and Thursday morning. At both meals, Jack actually *thanked* the execution team members and even offered each a share of his plate. When Jack entered the visitation yard on Thursday morning, he was not darkened. Like a child, he delighted in telling me how he offered execution team members part of the steak and chocolate cake, and we talked about why they might have turned down his kind offer.

Jack was more surprised when the warden delivered the last meal. Earlier on Thursday, he ordered fried chicken, French fries, and two cans of Coke. However, the warden presented Jack's meal with the added treat: a container of French onion soup. "Why warden, how did you know I love French onion soup? I haven't had it since I got here!" The warden just smiled and said he "heard a rumor." On his death day, perhaps for the first time in this life, Jack Trawick began to understand agape love and the good deeds that brought it forth.

The Start of a Conversation – A Good Deed

Once the warden left, as Jack enjoyed his last meal, we talked more about agape love. I reminded him how good he felt today and how bad he felt earlier in the week. Before 3:00 p.m., I caught Jack's attention to remind him about the importance of his last words in the execution chamber. It would be the start of a conversation concluding in front of God. I was frank: If it were me, I'd want that conversation to get off to a good start! He pondered for a moment, and then asked, "What should I say?" I paused, "That's between you and the Holy Spirit." I reminded him what he said when we first met several years ago – everything was "okay" between him and God. I encouraged Jack, it was not too late to renew that relationship.

Whose Father?

In accordance with Jack's preference, we had only one group prayer. It was the Lord's Prayer on his execution day. However, I asked Jack and his cousins for permission to alter the first line of the prayer. Rather than start with "*Our* Father who is in Heaven," we commenced with "*Jack's* Father who is in Heaven." After everyone recited the first altered line, I interrupted the prayer by asking, "Whose Father?" They responded, "Jack's

Father." I asked again, this time louder, "*Whose* Father?" They rejoined louder, "*Jack's* Father!" I repeated my question about 10 times until all were shouting and laughing, "*JACK's* Father who is in heaven!" Then we continued. It was important to remind Jack that, regardless of his deeds, God was still his God. After the prayer, the cousins grew still; one wept. The website operator no longer joked.

It was nearing the moment for Jack to return to the death cell – one final time. He hugged everyone. Kissed the female cousins on the cheek. Said in a twitching voice, "This is so surreal. I'm gonna be dead in two hours." But anger was absent.

Then Jack pulled me over and quietly asked two favors. First, I was to talk to the website operator about shutting down his "murder auction" business. "Tell him he can do more with his life. He's got a wife and kids. He doesn't need to be doing this." Second, I was to write to those nine teenage girls. As I would discover days after his execution, the second request was underscored in Jack's final letter I had yet to receive.[23] "Tell them, you're a friend of mine, and I want them to be exposed to another kind of life. Tell them it's stupid to get close to men like me. Don't send anyone pictures. Nothing good can happen. Tell them, there's a better life."

I Don't Deserve It, but I Do Ask for It

Jack was shackled and returned to the death cell around 4:30 p.m. He had a chance to shower and change into clean and freshly pressed prison clothes. He also had time to be alone with his own thoughts and, perhaps, prayer. As his spiritual advisor, I joined the chaplain and Jack in the death cell around 5:30 p.m.

Jack was now anxious. He repetitively stood and sat back down, and he fidgeted with his fingers. He soon muttered, "I'm ready. Let's go." The chaplain smiled compassionately and joked: "We ain't ready for ya, Jack! You're always in a hurry!" Jack started to calm down. We prayed and talked. The chaplain reminded him about John 11:26, "and whoever believes in me will never die. Do you believe this?" Jack affirmed he did believe. The chaplain reminded him again, every minute remaining in his life was an opportunity to heal others. I reminded him, his last words will conclude in a conversation with God. I urged Jack to follow the Holy Spirit and make that conversation sincere and authentic.

---

[23] In the letter I discovered these teenage girls lived throughout the world: one in Belgium, West Virginia, North Carolina, Minnesota, Connecticut, Tennessee, Wisconsin, and 2 from different cities in Australia.

With minutes remaining, Jack joked with the execution team members. He seemed to realize he was talking with friends. He ribbed them as being "knuckleheads" who someday may find "real jobs." Before he was extracted from the death cell, I hugged and kissed him on the cheek. I told him I loved him.[24] I reminded him, *his* Father is in heaven. He smiled, "yes."

A few minutes after 6 p.m., Jack Harrison Trawick was strapped onto the gurney.[25] I was in my place, and the witness curtains opened. Jack's last words:

> I wish to apologize to the people whom I have hurt, and I ask for their forgiveness. I don't deserve it, but I do ask for it.

Postmortem: Whom.

Who could speak grammatically before being executed? What other death row man would know to use *whom*? Jack's background afforded a privileged education, and that paid for his ability to articulate a good deed of healing in his last minute of life. I hoped it was a worthy start to a conversation that, as of 6:17 p.m., continued at the Foot of the Throne.

Expectations

Jesus never links *forgiveness* with *heaven*.[26] The Jesus-Loves-Me paradigm is crucial to knowing Christ, certainly a first step toward heaven, but the Jesus-Means-Business paradigm lays out the expectations for avoiding hell. Earlier, too, several assumptions were reviewed about Jesus' parables, especially those in Matthew 25. I hold no pretension to suggest God is bound to these expectations and assumptions, but they are linked to the professing of Jesus.

---

[24] In that last letter I had yet to receive, Jack Trawick wrote: "Thanks for the friendship… Love you, brother." He added a postscript, "Shower the people you love with love. Show them how you feel."

[25] Unbeknownst to Jack, a body bag laid under the bottom sheet so that, when it was over, he would be zipped up (sheets and all) and sent for autopsy at the University of South Alabama Hospital.

[26] As pointed out in Chapter 1, the purpose of forgiveness has never been a key to entry into heaven. Rather, forgiveness is an act of reconciliation with God to make the Christian authentic in the relationship with God. From forgiveness comes a rebirth of faith that enables the Holy Spirit to lead the Christian toward doing the good works and other expectations required for entry into heaven.

The Ten Virgins parable brings insight to one death row man – Jack Trawick – and his struggle with God's expectations and assumptions. Only God measures the outcome of this struggle. Jack's worry, as it should be yours and mine, was that no one but God knows the weight of each factor in the measurement.

Expectation 1

Jack was expected to do *good deeds.*

Expectation 2

Jack was expected to be *well-prepared* to do them.

Assumption A

Jack's preparation and alertness was to become *constantly (increasingly) heightened or expanded.* Good deeds this moment are assumed greater than last moment, yet less than the next moment.

Assumption B

The backbone of doing good deeds is the *Holy Spirit.* Without God's Spirit, Jack would not know where God needed the next good deed.

Assumption C

Each good deed was to *glorify God,* not Jack.

Assessment

Jack was the doer of evil deeds and, from this perspective, parabolic symmetry is skewed. Love was always unidirectional in his favor. His family loved him, but he never described them – even his parents – in loving ways. He never talked about family times where love may have flourished: Christmas, birthdays, even funerals. His cousins loved Jack sufficiently to disrupt their lives, travel to Atmore, visit with him for two days in a very disturbing setting, and then do the unimaginable – watch his execution. Yet he never indicated love for them. Jack did some good deeds on death row, but most of his deeds were not designed to benefit anyone but him.

In the free-world, Jack learned to manipulate. That kind of behavior usually lessens when the death row cell doors slam shut. Once confined alone 23 hours each weekday and 24 hours on weekends, others on the row did not have to "know him." Yet, the Marquis de Sade of the 21st century – *that monster* – devised postmodern patterns of infliction via letters and internet. Certainly for Jack, *hell was a process* not a result. The final product of evil never satisfied, but the process of doing evil brought *delicious, delicious delight*.

To give Jack the benefit of the doubt, he was not like everyone else. Diagnosed with mental illness before the evilest acts – murder – occurred, the illness included *homicidal impulses*. Nevertheless, a court judged Jack well enough to know right from wrong.

Impulses are not absolute. He might have become a paranoid schizophrenic, but God never created Jack as a murderer. The State of Alabama had the moral obligation to protect its citizens from predators like Jack but did nothing prior to the evil deeds. With the exception of his mother, family members did nothing. Jack could have committed himself to a mental health institution to deal with his sex deviancies a long time before the first murder victim, Betty Jo Richards. Yet he did not.

Not doing good deeds might be more inexcusable in Jack's case because, unlike others in the world, he had a good idea of when the Bridegroom would arrive. There was time to grasp God's hand as his lamp and use the Holy Spirit as his oil. Coming through the Holman gate, he knew the odds were never in favor of exiting alive. Jack had 15 years to prepare. He knew the precise day and time two months prior to dying. Well in advance, the chaplain explained the timing his death would take on execution Thursday.

Jack Trawick could not undo the evil acts of murder, but he never sought forgiveness for doing them. Reconciliation with his dead victims would have been the first step toward doing a good deed and becoming better-prepared to do more good deeds at a heighted constant, guided by the Holy Spirit, and dedicated to the glory of God. He never took ownership of why he was on death row. As with college and the military, in Jack's mind, he was always the exception.

Yet in that last 24 hours of life, Jack Trawick tried to do good. Monday's damning last words transfigured into Thursday's eloquent healing message. Perhaps he was covering his bets, but I saw a man about to meet God. Jack was like a child preparing for church; I felt he wanted to be clean and dressed to please *his* Father in heaven. The darkened world of Jack was losing the last battle, regardless of the war's outcome. Yes, *regardless of the war's outcome*, he began to choose the product of goodness over the process of evil.

Was Jack Trawick well-prepared to do the good deeds needed? No. He was ill-prepared. His last words were directed toward comforting the living but could not reconcile with the murdered. Jack *solicited* good deeds for the webpage operator and the nine teenage girls, yet he was ill-prepared to perform them himself. He understood the good deeds done by execution team members, but he was ill-prepared to comfort them about their one obligated task. He never made amends to his sister even after receiving the nephew's email on the morning of his execution. The idea of doing good came late in the game; he lacked time to spiritually heighten those deeds.

I believe Jack Trawick started to let the Holy Spirit guide him in his final letter to me. I think, in the death cell, it was not substantive food that made him aware of agape love. Rather, it was the good deed of generosity that allowed him to experience this kind of love through the Holy Spirit.

Yet it seemed Jack was most comfortable with transactional deeds and *quid pro quo* relationships. (This is why he never was truly friends with either the website operator or those nine teenage girls.) His spiritual comfort zone was a function of his own postmodern domestication of God. For Jack, hell was not Jesus' Gehenna Valley, although he did throw his victims into similar heaps. *Hell was a process,* and 21st century technology made that process (like Charles Manson's endeavors) easy, not difficult.

Precious Time

Did Jesus know Jack Trawick at that darkened door? The Jesus-Loves-Me paradigm begs us to think so. The Jesus-Means-Business paradigm brings doubt. Jack wasted so much precious time. Certainly he did good deeds (Expectation 1), but how much weight was allotted to so few good deeds? He did not seem well-prepared (Expectation 2). His good deeds heightened a little in the last hours (Assumption A), but the bar was set so low. I believe he was guided by the Holy Spirit (Assumption B). However, were his good deeds performed to glorify God (Assumption C), or were they a bail-out attached to an "anything goes" pass jammed in his front pocket?

Not Just Process but Choice

Jack told me a parable about a man who fell asleep and awoke as a newcomer in hell. He was given a tour of four places and told to choose one in which to stay for eternity. Three places were horrific, but the fourth had promise – men joyfully standing around and drinking coffee. All stood in feces up to their knees, but that appeared a lot more pleasant than the other options. "I choose to spend eternity here." As soon as he committed, Satan blew a whistle and shouted, "Your five minute coffee break is over for the next millennia. Then, no coffee. Just a chance to lay on the floor and sleep. But for now, everyone get back to standing on your heads!" Turned out, this place was most horrific.

The moral lesson: Be careful. You will never possess complete information. Still the choice is always yours, and yours alone.

Choice was certainly true of the five foolish women without oil. What about Jack Harrison Trawick?

The answer lies solely in the Hand of whom Trawick so often chose to shun. He continued to pick the process of hell even after knowing the exact day and hour of the Bridegroom's return. This made him much more foolish than the five foolish women.

If the Lord did not know him standing outside the Banquet Hall, it was because *that monster* chose not to be known. In a letter, Jack suggested he planted a thistle patch in life rather than a rose garden. And like the five foolish women, he may remain confined to a world so darkened. A world vacated by innocent sleep.

If that is the case, it was always Trawick's choice.

Yes, Jack's choice alone.

Chapter 3

Hell is a State of Mind –
On Either Side of the Barred Door

The Parable of the Talents

This chapter brings together the moral lesson found in the Parable of the Talents (Illustration 3.1) and a death row man, Jimmy Davis, Jr. Key verses are (1) Well done, good and faithful servant! You have been faithful with a few things; I will put you in charge of many things. (2) And throw that worthless servant outside, into the darkness, where there will be weeping and gnashing of teeth.

Illustration 3.1 The Parable of the Talents - Matthew 25:14-30

[14] "Again, it will be like a man going on a journey, who called his servants and entrusted his property to them. [15] To one he gave five talents, to another two talents, and to another one talent, each according to his ability. Then he went on his journey. [16] The man who had received the five talents went at once and put his money to work and gained five more. [17] So also, the one with two talents gained two more. [18] But the man who had received one talent went off, dug a hole in the ground and hid his master's money.
[19] "After a long time the master of those servants returned and settled accounts with them. [20] The man who had received the five talents brought the other five. 'Master,' he said, 'you entrusted me with five talents. See, I have gained five more.'
[21] "His master replied, 'Well done, good and faithful servant! You have been faithful with a few things; I will put you in charge of many things. Come and share your master's happiness!'
[22] "The man with two talents also came. 'Master,' he said, 'you entrusted me with two talents; see, I have gained two more.'
[23] "His master replied, 'Well done, good and faithful servant! You have been faithful with a few things; I will put you in charge of many things. Come and share your master's happiness!'

[24] "Then the man who had received the one talent came. 'Master,' he said, 'I knew that you are a hard man, harvesting where you have not sown and gathering where you have not scattered seed. [25] So I was afraid and went out and hid your talent in the ground. See, here is what belongs to you.'
[26] "His master replied, 'You wicked, lazy servant! So you knew that I harvest where I have not sown and gather where I have not scattered seed? [27] Well then, you should have put my money on deposit with the bankers, so that when I returned I would have received it back with interest.
[28] "'Take the talent from him and give it to the one who has ten talents. [29] For whoever has will be given more, and they will have an abundance. Whoever does not have, even what they have will be taken from them. [30] And throw that worthless servant outside, into the darkness, where there will be weeping and gnashing of teeth.'"

In the Talents parable, Jesus has two expectations: (1) use the talents God gives you and (2) use them righteously. Discussed in Chapter 1, there are three commonly accepted assumptions: talent must be (A) heightened or expanded; (B) guided by the Holy Spirit; and (C) used to glorify God (Morris, 1999; Turner, 2008).

The Moral Lesson

This is the moral lesson from the Parable of the Talents: Use talents righteously and you will avoid hell.

For more than 25 years, Jimmy Davis, Jr. has existed on death row. Will Jesus greet him as a good and faithful servant? Or will he be deemed *lazy* and cast to where there is weeping and gnashing of teeth. Will his use/abuse of talent impact the State's decision to kill him?

What is Talent?

To the ancient Greeks, a talent was a *weight* specified between 57 and 79 pounds (Arndt, et al., 2000:988). They also used it as a *monetary unit*; one talent equaled a specified *weight* in coins. In Jewish tradition, talent meant *acting righteously* (Levine & Brettler, 2017:57). Hiding or abusing one's talent was metaphor for not displaying virtue. To the early Christians, a talent was a *gift or ability* (Barker, 1995). You had talent if you could do something in an exceptional way. Hence, talent has four dimensions: it is a *gift* that is *weighted* heavily by the *coinage* of *righteous acts*. For Jews, Christians, and Muslims, it is a God-given gift.

The Barred Door – A Contemporary Parable

This is what hell is like. A man awakes, shaking in his tears. He cries softly so no one can hear him, but his weeping is uncontrollable during sleep. Awake or asleep, it doesn't matter; he lives the same nightmare – lying on a concrete slab in a small room with neither a chair nor a window to verify day and night. How did he get here? Where was he before? Memory fades.

Raucous chatter gushes through the barred door, the pitch and velocity of each voice competes with all others. The man responds, but no one cares what he says. Sweat soaks the sheets and shallow mattress. He begs sleep to delete the nightmare. He prays awakening finds him on the other side of the barred door. Yet nothing on the other side indicates the nightmare will abate. He is afraid but falls back asleep. Suddenly he hears a voice:

> Sloth! You were once a big shot but look at you now. Useless! Get your butt up. Do something for Me instead of you! Or truly I say, you will find nothing on either side of the barred door – nothing for eternity.

Hell is a *state of mind* where nothing but nightmare lies *on either side of the barred door*.

Meet Jimmy Davis, Jr.

Jimmy Davis, Jr. was born on October 6, 1970 at Mary-Michael Hospital in Harlem on New York City's Manhattan Island. His father is now

deceased. Jimmy has five sisters; two share his father. He is the second oldest in the Davis family.

Jimmy was a toddler when his parents divorced. The father moved to Detroit, and his mother brought Jimmy and his two sisters to Alabama. They relocated in Anniston where her grandmother and mother lived. Anniston is located in the Appalachian foothills between Birmingham and Atlanta on I-20. Built by the iron industry but unlike Birmingham, it remained a small community. Anniston's population is around 25,000, and 52 percent are black. Nearly 30 percent of the residents fall below the poverty line and only 20 percent are college educated (U.S. Census, 2020). Its impoverished streets would lead Jimmy Davis, Jr. to death row.

Because of his grandmother's drug addiction, Jimmy Davis' mother was raised by his great-grandmother. When the family returned to Alabama, they initially stayed with the great-grandmother on Gurnee Avenue. The street is anchored in a neighborhood of poor and low-income people. Jimmy's mother remarried and gave birth to three more daughters before that husband died. She worked several jobs, including as a cook and house cleaner, in an effort to make ends meet.

Several houses along Gurnee Avenue became home to the six Davis children. These were not large homes. The six children and mother had to fit into three tiny bedrooms, a small living room and kitchen, and one bathroom.

Talent of Brutality

Jimmy Davis' mother knew only one kind of discipline for her children: physical punishment (Whalen, 2013). Perhaps she learned this practice from her own drug-addicted mother, but her *talent of brutality* grew in severity. While the kids were still in diapers, slapping replaced scolding. Slapping turned into hitting and that transformed into beating. By the time Davis was 8 years old, the beatings were administered by either a broom handle or an electrical cord. The brutality assuredly had an emotional side. His mother would shout damning things, always comparing him to his "evil" father. Her words made him realize how little she loved him. He bears his father's name, and he grew up thinking he was also "evil" and had no value.

This perspective of childhood was not concocted by a death row man seeking sympathy or rendering excuse. The brutality was real. Jimmy Davis' sisters were also beaten, but he caught the brunt. A beating for Jimmy might last an intensive 20 minutes. At the age of seven, a beating resulted in a severe head injury and a distorted ear.

Talent of Lying

Welts and scars accumulated and led to the *talent of lying*. When teachers inquired, Jimmy Davis, Jr. said the sores were from falling off his bike. Children's Services eventually got involved, and right in front of Jimmy, his mother claimed his bruises were from tripping onto broken glass in a nearby dilapidated baseball field. Social workers tried unsuccessfully to amend her way of punishment, but the children never were removed from the mother's custody.

Talent of Self-Blame

The mother hurt him in multiple ways. According to Davis, "Women have to be careful with the words they use about their sons – it shapes how they feel." He believes the beatings were prelude to going down the wrong road in life. In the process, he learned the victim's *talent of self-blame*. He wanted so badly his mother's love but concluded the inability to get that love was his fault. Even today, he reflects on the struggle for his mother's love. "I went about it the wrong way. Not bringing home good grades but getting into trouble."

The Missing Talent of a Father

His father's family lived near Anniston, but his mother refused to let them visit. Davis' father wanted to pay child-support, but his mother refused all financial help from a man she insisted was evil. Hence, much of his developmental years were void of a father's presence – especially a father who offered love.

At the age of 16, Jimmy Davis, Jr. and one sister were permitted to visit their dad in Detroit. His father and stepmom gave them a loving vacation. Goodnight kisses and good morning hugs were abundant, and beatings were not part of their day. Jimmy, Sr. worked at a horse racetrack, and the kids accompanied him throughout the vacation. They helped with landscaping, but their dad made sure they got to pet the horses throughout the day. When they went home at night, their stepmom greeted them with home-cooked meals.

Unfortunately, their dad died from a heart attack during that visit. Jimmy Davis, Jr. recalls it was a "very confusing time. My mom wanted me and my sister to come home. My stepmom begged us to stay with her in Detroit." The kids chose to go back to Anniston. However, and this angered his mother, Jimmy decided to live with another sister's aunt. He gradually stayed with others in various houses on and near Gurnee Avenue: his great-grandmother, his best friend (Willie Smith) who lived in a nearby slum motel, and others who had a spare couch or a place on the floor. By this time, he had dropped out of school.

Talents of Trouble

Well before visiting his dad, at the age of 10, Jimmy's mother permitted him to hang out with his 20 year-old uncle. He liked this arrangement because it meant fewer beatings at home. However, his uncle "gave me not only bad advice but opened me up to a whole new world of petty crime and gangs." He developed the *talent to steal*. Bicycles were taken from backyards of homes on the other side of town. Jimmy and his friends would "ride them all day long, change parts off them to other bikes." Puppies were stolen through the rear side of a kennel and were sold on the same streets that produced the bikes.

Like his uncle, Jimmy Davis eventually developed the *talent of mentoring* – not the good kind of mentoring his father might have provided, but the bad kind: teaching ways to game the system and get what was desired. A male cousin and his little sister followed him. "I taught them how to fight, steal, and lie." The cousin "started messing with young girls just like I did and he ended up becoming a father at 15." This cousin "was so far in the streets, he never really formed a relationship with the mother or the baby." The infant grew up to be a teenage, single mother. In regard to Jimmy's little sister, she followed him into the world of gangs.

Gang Talent

At the age of 13, Jimmy Davis joined the Gangsta Disciples. He claims he thought gangs were a way to protect himself and the neighborhood. I suspect he wasn't that naïve. The Gangsta Disciples is a group, formed in Chicago, of young thugs who care nothing about who they hurt and which neighborhood stores they rob. "Black on black crime," Davis reflects on his experience in the Gangsta Disciples, "has crippled black communities in three ways: *drugs, death, and prison.*" The Gangsta Disciples contributed to the crippling of Anniston's poor neighborhoods. In this environment, he developed the *talent of planning* and the *talent of action* – talents that would end in drugs, death, and prison.

Jimmy Davis' initiation into the Gangsta Disciples occurred one night in an abandoned field across the street from his junior high school. "I got jumped by five brothers. I had to fight them for 60 seconds." From the start, he grew in leadership within the gang.

One day gang members talked about a young girl who wanted to join. Jimmy Davis said, "OK, tonight we'll do it." He describes the initiation. "So we met in the field. I saw it was my *youngest sister*." He tried talking her out of it as five male gang members encircled her, but his sister shouted, "I'm joining because you're in it!" Davis turned away not to see the 60-second gang-beating. "From that day forward, my sister stayed in trouble."

Gang activity led to crimes bigger than bicycles and puppies. In 1989, Davis phoned for a pizza delivery to an abandoned building. When the deliverer got out of the car, "We robbed him. No weapons at all. We all ran in different directions, but the police picked me up." Jimmy spent nine months in the county jail, and then two months in prison for third-degree felony. (This would prove consequential in his path to death row.)

The Talent of Murder

The Direct Oil station, at the corner of West 20th and Noble streets in Anniston, is now a car wash. Back in 1993, you could see this convenience store from the house at the corner of Gurnee Avenue and West 20th Street where Davis' mother lived. This was only two blocks from the service station, hence, he was very familiar with it.

According to court reports,[1] the robbery involved two adults – Jimmy Davis, Jr. and a gang member, Alphonso (Al) Phillips – and one minor, Al's 16 year-old cousin, Terrance Phillips. On March 17, 1993, Terrance joined the two adults to talk about a robbery. (As usual, alcohol and drugs were part of the meeting.) They developed a plan: Terrance would be the lookout, Davis would point the gun, and Al would grab the money.

That evening, they walked from Gurnee Avenue toward the Direct Oil station. Along the way, Terrance got cold feet and left. About 7:15 p.m., Davis and the older cousin approached the service station. With bandanas covering their faces, they saw attendant Johnny Hazel working alone and standing in the doorway. Davis allegedly raised a stolen .25 caliber Raven pistol and shouted, "Give it up, f___-nig___."[2] Hazel backed inside and either laughed or smiled in a way that triggered Davis. The Raven pistol discharged two bullets. Shocked at the gun's noise and the groans of a dy-

---

[1] Information about the murder and conviction comes from *Court of Criminal Appeals of Alabama*, 1995; *Court of Criminal Appeals of Alabama*, 2006; *Jimmy Davis – Alabama Death Row*, 2017; *Supreme Court of Alabama*, 1998.

[2] The .25 caliber Raven is a relatively ineffective weapon. It is not designed to hunt animals, nor is it a good self-defense weapon. Its street value is its inexpensive price. A used Raven in 1993 was worth about $30. See Genitron.com, 2020.

ing man, Jimmy Davis and Al Phillips forgot the money and darted down West 20th Street toward Gurnee Avenue. An autopsy showed Johnny Hazel was hit in the right chest and the left side of his back.

A Talent of Boasting

Several witnesses heard the shots from their homes and saw two black men running down the street. They could not identify Jimmy Davis, Jr. or Al Phillips, but Davis had a mouth to match his swagger. According to testimony, he bragged to several friends, including his best friend Willie Smith and Smith's several girlfriends, about what he said to Johnny Hazel and what he did after Hazel laughed or smiled. "Man, I shot that f___-nig___. I shot him... *The second time felt even better than the first.*" Davis boasted, "I wasn't going to let no cracker laugh at me." Of course, these conversations happened only if his friends were telling the truth.

The Talent of Covering Butt

There was one talent Jimmy Davis never acquired: the talent of disloyalty. He assumed his gang members would remain loyal. He thought Willie Smith would do the same. He bet the Phillips cousins would not cut a deal. Jimmy Davis was wrong on all fronts. Everyone but Davis covered their butts.

Police found the gun at Al Phillips' house, and ballistics matched the bullets and shell casings to that gun. According to Davis, his appointed lawyer never requested fingerprints. Arrests were made several days after the murder, and the "prisoner's dilemma" went into effect (Paterson, 2015).[3] The three were placed in separate interrogation rooms. Since Jimmy Davis, Jr. boasted about killing Johnny Hazel, detectives approached the Philipps cousins to flip them against Davis. They entered into plea agreements. For testifying against Davis, each received a reduced sentence – ten years for first degree conspiracy to commit robbery.

---

[3] The prisoner's dilemma occurs in crimes where each participant had unequal share in the outcome of murder. The dilemma is to stay loyal or be the first to strike a deal for a lighter sentence recommendation.

The Trial

No state in the U.S. sends a murderer to death row. There must be aggravating factors that merit capital murder.[4] The State filed a capital charge against Davis because of two aggravating factors. (1) The murder took place in the process of robbery. (2) Davis was already a convicted felon because of the pizza deliverer robbery. Davis never testified, which is not unusual in criminal cases, and his attorney tried unsuccessfully to discredit the witnesses whom Davis thought were his friends. He was convicted of murder.

Sentencing

Capital cases in the U.S. are divided into two segments: the trial (guilty/not guilty) phase and the sentencing phase. In the latter, the State and defendant bring witnesses to convince the jury to recommend either the maximum capital sentence (the death penalty), a moderate sentence (life-without-parole) or a more lenient verdict (life with the chance of parole).

At sentencing, family members and friends of Johnny Hazel testified for the State. As for Jimmy Davis, he learned another lesson about loyalty. No members of the Gangsta Disciples testified on his behalf. No neighbor on Gurnee Avenue pleaded for his life. His mother and a cousin testified but according to Davis, his lawyer did not prepare them. Neither pled he was innocent, a customary practice during sentencing by many mothers despite the guilt having already been rendered. They told the jury of Davis' turbulent upbringing – the brutal beatings and the devastating impact of losing his dad. However, rather than begging for the lenient sentence of life with the possibility of parole, both urged for *life-without-parole*. In a vote of 11-1, the jury recommended the maximum penalty: death.

Allocution

Perhaps the allocution was just an insincere effort to gain sympathy. It was probably written by Davis' lawyer, who might have used the same wording time and time again. Yet maybe his allocution was an honest presentation of fact. From the start, Jimmy Davis, Jr. claimed he was at an aunt's house when the crime was committed. Prior to the judge rendering a decision, he allocuted:

---

[4] Aggravating factors can differ from state to state. However, they typically include murdering a pregnant woman or murdering a police officer, in addition to committing murder during the commission of a theft and murder by an assailant who is previously convicted of a felony.

Judge, I'm innocent... And I'm very sorry for Mr. Hazel and I would like to apologize to the family members and everything, but it wasn't me...

On December 10, 1993, the judge accepted the jury's recommendation of execution. Jimmy Davis, Jr. was going to death row at the age of 23.

The Journey to Death Row

Immediately after the judge pronounced sentence, Davis began to realize the use of his talents that got him this far in life were not going to save him from execution. He felt powerless, and his first instinct was not survival but suicide. Even in the court building, "I was going to make the police kill me." Two officers walked him to the courthouse lobby to await transportation to the Calhoun County jail. He kept eyeing their revolvers and tried to think of how he could "grab one of their guns to make them shoot me to death." Shackled, he no longer had that kind of power.

On March 4, 1994, Jimmy Davis, Jr. changed from the county jail orange garb into the clothes he wore at trial. He was transported from the county jail in Anniston to Holman Prison in Atmore. The distance travelled was about 225 miles. The leg from Anniston to Montgomery entailed winding two-lane roads before the Sheriff's car connected to I-65 for the second part of the trip. The ride took a little more than four hours.

In the car, Davis continued to grasp the notion of being powerless. Shackled, he needed help getting into the backseat. He remained cuffed and shackled throughout the ride, which meant he could not control the air vent or crack the window. Pulling out of the county jail, his last view of Anniston turned quickly into open rolling hills, pastures, and small communities. Davis realized he had no control over seeing Anniston again.

No conversation in the car included Jimmy Davis. He just did not matter because he had no value – much like how his mother made him feel. Within the stream of country music, the officers talked about college football spring training and whether Alabama or Auburn would win the Iron Bowl in the fall. Jimmy Davis loves college football, it is his greatest passion, but he could not interject his opinions – not even about football. He was a death row man.

The final leg of the trip, exiting I-65 in Atmore, is a short ride. Coming down Ross Road to Holman, Davis saw the last of farming fields, open skies, and small wooded conclaves. All that ended as the car came up the other side of a gully, and to his right, was the prison. Built in 1969 with a capacity of around 1,000, Holman in 1994 held approximately 2,000 inmates including around 200 on death row.[5] Having gone through the sally-gate in the rear of the prison, the car stopped. Helping Davis out of the car, one officer (who Davis thought was rough with him in the county jail) stared and said, "Be strong." Davis wondered how he could be strong when he was powerless. He was now in the custody of Holman's COs, and none of his talents worked.

Death Row

Holman's death units consist of 7 rows, each with two tiers. On each tier are 14 single cells. Walking toward Holman's rear entrance doors, still shackled, Jimmy Davis, Jr. unknowingly passed the death cell and the death chamber. He was escorted to booking where he exchanged his trial garments for Alabama DOC all-white clothes: a shirt with his Z number etched on the front corner, pants, socks, shoes, cap, underwear, sweatshirt, and white jacket.[6] He was also given a drinking cup, a toothbrush, a towel, a pencil, several sheets of paper, carbon paper to copy what he writes to his lawyer, and a box containing his court records.

Still shackled, Davis had to manage carrying everything as he was moved to a death row cell. The barred door slammed shut. He was now on Z-1 status, and typical of all men in that situation, powerlessness sunk in deeper.[7]

---

[5] Overflow for death row is handled in two ways: (1) there is a men's satellite death row at Donaldson prison, near Birmingham, or (2) other segregation cells are used at Holman.

[6] Z number: Alabama general population inmates, upon arrival, receive an identification number, the Alabama Institutional Serial (AIS) number. This six-digit number indicates the order in which prisoners have entered the system. Condemned inmates, however, receive a three-digit ID number with the prefix of Z. Using the last letter in the alphabet is reflective of their status in the system and society (Slack, 2009). W. Virgil Murphy earned Z-001, and he was executed in 1927. Z-577 is the ID number assigned to Jimmy Davis, Jr., which means he was the 577th man to enter death row.

[7] Z-1 status. The initial period on death row is spent in isolation until it can be determined how a death row man will behave. Usually that period is 30-45 days. Like all death row inmates, Davis was in his cell for 23 hours a day. But unlike the rest, he would remain in segregation even for the one hour of relief. It's called "walk-alone;" he was placed in an individual cage to "walk" outside. There might be another new inmate on Z-1 status in a nearby cage, but no personal contact.

First Night

I know of no man who is not devastatingly anxious on the first night on death row. It's easy for free-world people to misunderstand: no one starts their day with the intent to murder someone in such a way as to end up on death row. So that first night, and many thereafter, most death row men harbor wishes about putting that bullet back into the gun's barrel and never discharging it in the first place. Even if a man previously served time in general population, like Davis for robbing the pizza deliverer, the experience on death row is unique. Afterall, it is *death* row, and there is nothing you can do about it. Most cry, perhaps for the first time in their lives. Yet like most tough guys, Davis tried to hide his tears behind an expressionless *game-face* – a talent common in prison, but his was crafted under his mother's beatings. Like the contemporary parable – *The Barred Door* – death row men come to realize on the first night that this confinement is like no other. Jimmy Davis, Jr. realized this too.

Davis' memory is blurred about much of that first night – a common psychological defensive mechanism of death row inmates. He remembers the 8'x5' walls closing in. His thin mattress. A combination toilet and sink with only a metal plate for a mirror. A blanket, pillow, and sheets. He remembers constant chatter. Early in the night, he tried to join in but no one listened. No one cared. He had no TV, but others did and those blared to compete with the chatter.

Davis' sleep was interrupted by tears, thoughts of anger and desire for revenge toward friends who testified against him and cousins cutting deals, and overwhelming anxiety about his claim of innocence being discarded. He wanted desperately to wake from this nightmare. Despite it being March and no death row cell had heat, Davis sweat profusely – soaking his bed. He woke up hoping he was still on Gurnee Avenue, but he wasn't. Asleep or awake, the nightmare was just beginning. A nightmare of incapacity. A nightmare of looming death.

Life on the Row

Jimmy Davis, Jr. once told me, "You wouldn't like me my first ten years here." In fact, "you're better off never coming close to me." Prison officials agree. He tried to use talents learned on Gurnee Avenue. He did not trust anyone. He lied about everything. He tried to bully his way among the other death row men and the COs.

Davis admits having been "mad, angry, and even immature." He told me, "I didn't care how I acted. I hated those who put me here." During the daily one-hour exercise period, he tried to employ talents taught by his uncle and refined in the gang: lie, steal, boast, manipulate.

Davis fought a lot. Once in the death row yard, he attacked another condemned man for saying something. Similar to the situation with Johnny Hazel, Davis didn't even hear him clearly. He just assumed what was said belittled him. Unlike the time with Johnny Hazel, he had only his body as a weapon. "It was a fist attack. Me and him stayed enemies until his execution."

At every turn, Davis opposed the COs. He almost got into a fight with a CO on one shake-down of his cell. The CO found a stash of ten rolls of toilet paper.[8] Davis threatened the CO, and fortunately, another CO stepped in and calmed him. The toilet paper was nevertheless confiscated from his cell.

The bottom line is Jimmy Davis, Jr. "blamed everyone for my imprisonment." There was no learning curve. "If you did approach me, I was always thinking you had an agenda." Lack of control over everything except bowel movements made the first decade on death row even more unbearable than it was designed to be. I believe he hoped somehow to get killed to end the nightmare. I know he pondered suicide, but lacking overhead cell bars, it seemed he could not figure how to take his life.[9] Enraged, he never accepted blame for his own actions. He just held tight to his *state of mind* – the nightmare of hell from which there was no escape.

Escape

If you met Jimmy Davis, Jr. today, he would tell you he escaped that hellish *state of mind* only when he surrendered all power to God. He likes to say, "I died for Christ and got off death row." He quickly adds, "Now it's *Life Row* for me!" But it was a struggle to find positive use of God's talents, and so the discovery of Life Row did not happen overnight.

---

[8] Because each inmate gets only one roll each week, toilet paper is of tremendous value on the prison black market (Slack, 2009). He probably convinced another CO to sneak him the toilet paper and was trying to make deals with other death row men.

[9] Jimmy would eventually learn how suicide occurs in cells with no bars on the ceiling. You take your belt or sheet, tie one end around your neck and the other to the barred door. You lie on your knees facing away from the bar so that the belt or sheet begins to cut off circulation. You must remain in that position after you pass out. It is difficult to strangulate yourself, but it is accomplished too many times on death row.

Kairos

There are many Christian ministries in prisons. The Kairos prison ministry is similar to the free-world spiritual movements of Cursillo or Emmaus.[10] Kairos is interdenominational, and therefore, does not try to lead participants (called "pilgrims") into a particular sect (Kairos, 2020). Participation is not restricted to Christians, and hence, conversion is not overtly pushed. The doctrine of Kairos is simple: "Listen, Listen, Love, Love." Free-world volunteers do not know the crimes committed by the pilgrims. They come to the prison to visit Jesus (Matthew 25:36). It is a Kairos tradition, given the standard routine of prison food, to bring in home-cooked meals and a lot of home-baked cookies. These are made and served as if the recipients – pilgrims and COs -- are, in fact, Jesus.

The number of inmates participating in a Kairos weekend is a function of available space for small-group tables.[11] Open space on Holman's death row can fit only 12 inmates and a handful of free-world volunteers. The prison chaplain selects the inmates, and on death row, every inmate is eventually invited. At the end of the weekend, many testify they originally came for the food. Yet they also confess receiving much more spiritual nourishment than was expected. Perhaps for the first time in their lives, they see free-world men without *game-faces*, just having fun, acting like children, and praising God. The inmates begin to realize they, too, can rid themselves of game-faces – at least on a Kairos weekend. They begin to understand they landed on death row because they were acting child*ish* in love of worldly desires rather than acting child*like* in love of God.

Ten years into his time on death row, Jimmy Davis was selected by the chaplain. Like others, he came for the food and wore his game face. Like others, he was surprised Kairos volunteers presented no pressure to take

---

[10] The Roman Catholic Cursillo movement started after WWII with the shortage (because of war-related deaths) of young lay leaders. Cursillo is Spanish for "short course" – a short course on Christ and the Holy Spirit. The Methodists Emmaus movement, similar to Cursillo, started in the 1960s as a way to revitalize lay leadership. Other denominations have similar spiritual movements. Their purpose is to provide an environment where the intimacy of God can be felt by the participant. Using the intense weekend format, these movements are led by volunteer laypeople. The weekend consists of 15 short talks, small group discussions, praise music, and a lot of food!

[11] Typically there are seven tables, each with six inmates, two free-world facilitators, and one table chaplain. There are usually more than 20 other free-world men in the talk room. Hence, a total of 42 inmates and around 40 free-world volunteers.

any faith-steps. He found the short talks relevant to his plight on death row, and the small group discussions were non-judgmental. If anything, Jimmy was shocked at free-world men laughing and talking with inmates. They expected nothing in return. They respected the Muslims and those who felt the Christian faith had abandoned them long before death row. The free-world men talked intimately about their lives, and they seemed genuinely caring about the life of each death row man.

Like many inmates, Davis was in tears to discover his paper placemats for each meal were drawn, colored, and signed by different children and each crayoned a note: "I love you" or "God loves you and so do I!" Jimmy also cried discovering people around the world were praying for him – by name – in 30 minute time slots throughout the weekend. Tears also flowed because of the agape love given by one woman who, like the children placemat "artists" and adult prayer warriors, neither Davis nor the other death row men would ever meet to thank. This lady's only son was murdered on Mother's Day eve. Since then, she routinely makes the best fudge brownies for Holman death row Kairos. She told me, "I do it because Michael is now with Jesus, and you're visiting Jesus on death row."

Agape love, discussed in Chapter 1, is love so great it can never be repaid. With all this agape love, Jimmy Davis' game-face fell to the side.

The short talks on Saturday focused on the topic of *forgiveness*. In small group discussions, inmates and volunteers were encouraged to write down names or titles of people each needed to *forgive*. The small groups talked about the difficulty of having to forgive others and the struggle to forgive *themselves*.

Death row men tend to feel they are beyond forgiveness. Yet, until that Kairos weekend, Jimmy Davis, Jr. never viewed himself as someone needing forgiveness. After all, he would tell you, "I'm not to blame." To be forgiven means you have done something wrong. Davis, remember, claims he is innocent.

Nevertheless, his list grew throughout that Saturday – and he found his name at the top. He admitted needing forgiveness for many things. "I misled a lot of young men into the life of gangs, drugs, and drinking." He was sorry for letting his little sister become a gang member. He was remorseful for hating his best friend and every other person who testified or cut deals against him. He even listed the district attorney, the jury, the judge, and everyone who Davis felt did him wrong while on death row. His list grew as the afternoon continued!

Kairos Saturday evenings are dedicated to ceremonially surrendering the burden of hate through forgiveness. This is done by each person destroying the list of people who they needed to forgive. In general population Kairos, that ceremony typically occurs outside where the lists are burned. In Holman's death row, men cannot go outside and burning inside is prohibited. The lists, therefore, are written on special paper that dissolves when placed in a bowl of warm water. After praying on his knees for each name, Jimmy surrendered the list and watched the paper dissolve.

The Kairos ministry tosses seeds: some will grow and others may not. After the weekend, Jimmy Davis, Jr. went back to his old, routine life on death row. However, seeds began taking root. He started attending – occasionally at first but eventually every Sunday – the Life Row church. His behavior gradually changed and inmates and COs took notice.

Encounters with Goodness

A man from New Jersey started writing him. He visited Jimmy one Friday and stayed in a nearby hotel to continue the visit on Monday. These were not "godly visits" in the sense that neither talked about faith. They were, however, *encounters with goodness*. As Jimmy eventually realized, "when our souls are wounded, we can never have vision of God's goodness." Because his soul was still wounded, Davis did nothing but complain to this man – four hours on Friday and four hours on Monday.

Nevertheless, the man from New Jersey continued to write and show agape love. He sent Jimmy food packages and put money into Jimmy's allowance account. Yet Jimmy remained unaware of this man's sacrifice and love. The man eventually stopped writing because of an illness and then the passing of his wife. But from that first encounter of goodness, Jimmy learned three lessons: (1) "never take for granted the sacrifices made for you;" (2) never miss "your moment" – "I never really thanked him;" and (3) "if he did not get removed from my life, that man would have been my provider, not Jesus." The third point was most important. It led Jimmy to seek a permanent provider – God.

No Longer Useless to the Lord

Months after the Kairos weekend, Jimmy was baptized in the Life Row church. Since then, he has had five mentors on death row. Pete encouraged him to read the bible and to be active in a bible study group. Anthony, like Jimmy, was a gang member with a very rough past. "He showed me how to be accountable to others that you have influence with." From Melvin, he saw what peace can do. "I never seen this place affect his witness." Jeffrey was an example to Jimmy. "One day someone fouled him hard on the basketball court and he did not come after him! I wanted to know where that strength came from, and he told me 'Jesus'." Greg pushed Jimmy to use his talent. "I was just going to church but, Greg told me I was going to preach *next* Sunday. I was so scared but I did it." Jimmy preached on what he learned in Kairos, *forgiveness*.

With the help of these mentors, Jimmy developed his talent to be a leader – not in a gang sense – but in the Life Row church. It marked the beginning of listening to God – listening with *lost ears* – and obediently developing talents that were hidden so deeply on Gurnee Avenue. The entire death row became his Life Row, and it was Jimmy's place of work. He learned to read, write, and speak – not like a useless gang leader in Anniston – but with useful righteousness in word and action.

A Score of 77

All this is even more miraculous when you realize Jimmy Davis, Jr. has a low IQ – *borderline intellectual disability*. Before his trial, the defense arranged for an intelligence diagnostic test, and the result was presented in the trial before sentencing.[12] Borderline intellectual disability ranges from 70 to 84. His score was 77. He has an IQ rating at the 6th percentile. That is, 94 percent of people his age have a higher IQ score. Jimmy Davis, Jr. functions at the 5th grade level.

Life Row Talents

You may think otherwise, but I believe God is doing it. Oh, it could be by chance or maybe just boredom from confinement in a small death row cell. But I think chance or boredom has nothing to do with it. I have known countless death row men who were bored, and some cast their lot by chance. Yet none have developed talents like Jimmy Davis, Jr.

History records many people with afflictions who develop amazing talents. Despite having a stuttering disability, Moses led a nation. Lincoln spoke profoundly the "Gettysburg Address" regardless of his annoying high-pitched voice. Saint Teresa of Calcutta persuaded many that Jesus was every poor person at her doorstep – her faith made a difference despite being a tiny female confronted by an extremely male-dominated culture.

---

[12] Though the Supreme Court had not yet ruled on the issue of executing persons with mental disabilities, defense teams around the country were introducing it at sentencing. Jimmy Davis' lawyer did the same. In 2002 the Supreme Court ruled that executing persons with intellectual disabilities violates the 8th Amendment's protection against cruel and unusual punishment. See *Atkins v. Virginia*, 2002.

Fact is, it's not just the famous who overcome disability to develop and use talent. With a 77 IQ, Jimmy Davis, Jr. is one such person. Talents honed on Gurnee Avenue – lying, cheating, bullying, taking – all proved unsuccessful on death row. Jimmy now turned to talents of righteousness. He turned to talents that glorify God. And much changed.

1 a.m. Wake-up Call

Jimmy once asked me, "Do you know where I am?" I responded, "You're in prison, my friend. You're sitting with me in this sweltering room called the visitation yard." He smiled, "No. I'm not! I'm in Christ, not prison." I then poked, "Well, how the hell did you get out of prison?" Jimmy's smile grew, "I heard God's voice at 1 a.m., and he wouldn't let me go back to sleep. He said, *'Don't be lazy today! Do something useful in My name.'* And I'm too excited to be hot or tired this afternoon! I'm no longer useless in here." God led him to Isaiah 50:4:

> The Sovereign LORD has given me an instructed tongue, to know the word that sustains the weary. He wakens me morning by morning, wakens my ear to listen like one being instructed.

In the middle of the night, God promised Jimmy he would sleep well and awake each morning with instruction.

The Talent of Reading

If you visit inmates, you know never to get into a bible-challenge – especially with death row men. They have plenty of time to read, and bibles are pro bono in any prison. If you frequent a prison, you probably find two types of bible-readers: those who memorize so they can arrogantly display their knowledge and those who read and earnestly apply scripture to the context of their lives and the lives of others. This latter group typically invites engagement with what they read. Jimmy fits here. For someone who never read a book in school, Jimmy began reading the Bible – all of it, repeatedly – to become engaged with God and with others.

Just for fun, Jimmy often includes a bible question in his correspondence. "Moses went to Egypt and told pharaoh what to do. Pharaoh couldn't put him in bondage, but he had all the children of Israel placed in bondage. Why?" Or "How many times was David anointed?" Or "How is Ruth connected to Jesus?" He never gives the answer but offers clues. His point is not to boast his knowledge but to bless me (and others) with the word of God.

Each time we visit, Jimmy's talent of reading enables him to fill the four hours with applied scripture. Regardless of topic, scripture is used to explain, analyze, or suggest remedy. And believe me, it is never boring! Even when we discuss the most important of topics – Jimmy's great love of American college football – he uses verses to help cope with why his beloved University of Miami Hurricanes suffer another losing season (e.g., 2 Timothy 2:5), or why my beloved Ohio University Bobcats will never – *never*, Jimmy likes to emphasize – win a national championship (e.g., Philippians 2:3)![13] Jimmy laughs, "It's all in scripture, brother!"

The Talent of Listening

There was a time when Jimmy listened only to himself. For more than 15 years, he has practiced the Kairos motto of "listen, listen, love, love." Patiently and intensely, he seeks God's daily instruction.

Conversations and correspondences often start with a question: "Guess what God told me today?" Then he answers, God says He wants me to… "stay in peace despite my disappointments"… "respond to others with *courage*"… "not confuse what I'm living *on* and what I'm living *for*." God told Jimmy not to worry because "He is covering my heart, not condemning my heart." Filled with exuberance, he once came into the visitation yard with the news: "God told me last night to go to sleep with a smile on my face because He is changing my story." Jimmy is certain God has pronounced him innocent.

He applies the talent of listening to others on death row. The COs have appointed him a tier "runner" – and this is an honor. From 4 a.m. to 4 p.m., Jimmy is out of his cell to serve the needs of others on his tier. This entails microwaving hot water for those making coffee in the cells, distributing cups of ice to combat the summer heat and humidity, and serving food trays to both tiers of his row – breakfast at 4 a.m., lunch at 10 a.m., and dinner at 3 p.m.

Jimmy uses his role as runner to engage in a *ministry of listening*. Other death row men have come to trust him. All of them are afraid, not of Jimmy any longer, but of their own self-made circumstance. Many are angry. Some still try to game the system as they did on the streets. Most receive no contact from free-world people after about 18 months. Loved-ones die

---

[13] 2 Timothy 2:5 - Similarly, anyone who competes as an athlete does not receive the victor's crown unless he competes according to the rules. Philippians 2:3 - Do nothing out of selfish ambition or vain conceit, but in humility consider others better than yourselves.

and they hear about it perhaps months later. Wives divorce them. They are lonely. Depression sets in.

Jimmy listens and offers the love of God. He never divulges names but will ask me hypotheticals about someone to whom he is ministering. "I need to ask you an important question"... "Have you ever been disconnected emotionally from [your wife]? What got you reconnected"... "How would you talk to someone thinking about suicide?"

Jimmy listens to me and many free-world people who write him. Once after reading all my gripes about work and stress, he comforted me, "The quality of your life and the quality of your decisions will be determined by who you spend the most time with – your family or your job. Which is it going to be, brother?"

His talent for listening extends beyond being a runner. An avid volleyball player, Jimmy listens to how death row men react to winning and losing. He cheers up men in between games. He also has a "fence ministry." He stands next to an outer fence and listens to concerns of other death row men and then leads all in praising God for the blessings they have. COs commonly gravitate and join in the praise celebration.

There are COs who trust Jimmy to the point of turning to him with personal problems. Jimmy is quick to remember, "The 'police' are also imprisoned here, just like me."[14] Some share their concerns about family or health issues. One CO, also a pastor of a church in Atmore, talks to Jimmy about sermons and scriptures. Jimmy laughs, "He'll even steal my sermons to use in his own church!"

When he hears arguments brewing, Jimmy intervenes to bring peace. He writes:

> A brother came out to work the halls with me Thursday. He came out complaining and then he started speaking his anguish and bitterness towards some brothers on his tier. I told him to stop focusing on them and focus on serving the Lord but he kept speaking negative which poisons the atmosphere on his tier. I finally told him to go get some sleep because I knew he was up all night. He did and I took over his tier. I tried to correct the poison by spreading my love to help them. I saw the other brother later that day and he had a good sleep. He thanked me. When I spread joy and love, I get more in return.

---

[14] The COs' work environment is stressful with long hours and few days off. They, too, are without air-conditioning or heat.

The Talent of Giving

I am allowed to bring $40 in quarters for vending machines each time I visit Jimmy.[15] I usually purchase several types of hot sandwiches, fruit juices, candy bars, and several slices of Jimmy's favorite from the vending machine, key lime pie. Everything is on our table as he walks in, and so are the remaining quarters. I consider the quarters as my tithing to prison ministry, and Jimmy knows those quarters are his to glorify God.

Jimmy knows which inmates have visitors who cannot afford to bring many quarters. Because inmates are not allowed to leave their chairs in the visitation yard, he frequently asks me to retrieve things from the vending machines for specific people in the room. He also asks me to take one or more of his sandwiches to someone. It is a tradition for him to make sure every visiting child gets a candy bar. Oh, their smiles warm your heart! If food remains on our table at the close of visitation, he reminds me to give those items to the COs.

On a visitation right before Mother's Day, Jimmy used the quarters to pay for photos of each man and mom visiting that day.[16] Then he instructed each man to give that picture to his mom, saying, "Happy Mother's Day." Sometimes conversations between family and condemned men are difficult, but because of Jimmy's expression of agape love that day, the entire room suddenly exploded with joy. Mothers started singing hymns and everyone joined in. One CO was in tears as she, too, joined in song while monitoring the room. I should note Jimmy's mother has visited him only once, more than 20 years ago.

To death row men and COs, Jimmy typically reinforces a conversation by giving the person, later in the day, a relevant scripture written on a small piece of paper. He gives his coffee (purchased with allowance money) to others in need. Whatever food packages are sent to him by free-world people, he shares with everyone on his tier.

When he sees a CO, he thanks the officer for blessing his day. They smile and feel somewhat better – given the challenges faced each day. Typical of many, I heard one CO in the visitation yard respond, "No, Jimmy. Thank *you* for blessing *my* day."

---

[15] The food in those machines, though outrageously overpriced, is different than what is served each day.

[16] Routinely the opportunity to purchase a photo with a guest is offered by a CO toward the end of each visit.

The Talent of Prayer

Prayer is important to everyone. Atheists may call it "hoping" and secularists may call it "thoughts." Regardless, everyone can relate to wanting or needing something so badly they seek a remedy or a miracle. John Calvin reminds us to pray with a sense of (1) reverence, (2) need and repentance, (3) humility and trust in God, and (4) confident hope (Keller, 2015: 97-107).[17]

Jimmy may not know Calvin, but he comes pretty close to adhering to the four rules. He takes prayer very seriously. He is humble, repentant, trusts God, and is always *confident in hope*. In fact, confident hope has led him, through prayer, to be convinced God has another plan for him – a plan other than execution.

I have prayed with Jimmy countless times: for hours when we have been in charge of a Kairos weekend prayer chapel (a vacant death row cell), during the last 30 minutes of each four-hour visit, in our letters, and over the phone. His prayers incorporate many – including the state's governor and attorney general, Holman's warden, the prison chaplain, the COs working death row, family members of death row men who are in need, death row men who face execution, and the loved-ones of death row men who commit suicide.[18]

His confidence in hope shows the fun he and God have with prayer. Jimmy prays for food he has never tasted. He never tells anyone (except me) what food he is praying for. Sometimes it takes a year or more, but he confidently waits for its arrival – by one of the death row COs who "mistakenly" bought an extra take-out lunch. This is how he got a taste of fried shrimp, sautéed gizzards, Chinese food, cheesecake, carrot cake, and pork chops!

When he comes into the visitation yard wearing a special smile, I know a food prayer was answered. Jimmy starts with, "James, why didn't you tell me about…?" Or "James, have you ever eaten …?" Then he describes every bit of joy he experienced eating whatever it is. When it came to cheesecake, his prayers were rewarded ten-fold. A CO said there was a party and one complete cheesecake was left. Jimmy shared it at the next Life Row gathering. Sometime later, he received an entire carrot cake,

---

[17] But even Calvin admits God may not reject prayer if these four rules are broken.

[18] Even the son of one of his pen pals committed suicide. Not only did Jimmy pray on his knees and through letters for her, but he also developed a friendship with the boy's father and prayed with him, too.

which he also shared with others. All this through the talent of prayer. A talent he did not acquire until his 10th year on death row.

The Talent of Writing

A lot of people cannot write. Many educated people cannot write.[19] It is a miracle that Jimmy Davis, Jr. has developed the talent of writing. It hasn't been easy. I remember the first letter I received, back around 2005, was barely interpretable. It was written by a man reflecting an IQ score of 77, who dropped out of the 9th grade, and had the intellectual capacity of a 5th grader. My responding letter simply could not address whatever he tried to write. This continued, but gradually I saw a change in his writing. Sure there remain grammatical errors, but his points are clear and robust. In a recent letter:

> You know I love watching football. My favorite play is the long touchdown pass. Every time I see one, a defender got out of assignment and lost focus. That's just like us Christians. We get out of focus and fail to bear witness to others at work and in our lives.

His talent developed to such a degree I invited him to write a devotional for *The Christian Public Servant* – an internet-based workday devotional that, between 2012 and 2018, went to over 40,000 daily readers in the public and nonprofit sectors around the world. At first, Jimmy balked at the idea, saying he would have to pray about it. A couple of weeks passed and I received his response, "God is directing me to do this. He made me rethink my situation. Life Row is where I work. This is where I work for God." Soon Jimmy wrote every Friday's devotional for *The Christian Public Servant*.

Each workday's devotional was distributed electronically around 4 a.m. Yet sometimes we did not get it out on time. When we were late sending Friday's out, emails would soon flood in from across the world asking if there was anything wrong with Jimmy. (My graduate assistants and I could all be dead, but the concern was always for Jimmy!) In the six years of daily publication, hundreds of emails came testifying how much Jimmy's workplace stories helped in both job and career. Illustration 3.2 contains Jimmy's first devotional.[20]

---

[19] Frankly, it plagues the academy and publishers know this.

[20] As with all submitted pieces to *The Christian Public Servant*, editing was required for Jimmy's submissions. Yet many individuals, far up the IQ ladder, required consistently more editing than did his weekly contribution.

Illustration 3.2 Jimmy Davis' first devotion, titled *At the Heart* (Slack, et al., 2015)

Reading: 1 Samuel 16:7 But the Lord said to Samuel, "Don't judge by his appearance or height, for I have rejected him. The Lord doesn't see things the way you see them. People judge by outward appearance, but the Lord looks at the Heart.

Reflection: I am in prison – on death row.

Since arriving here, God has brought many people into my life. A warden and chaplain who follow Christ each day. Many guards are truly amazing Christians. There are free-world volunteers who visit so often, bringing Christian fellowship and the promise of the Word. You may be surprised, but the Body of Christ is alive and well where I live. You may call it death row, and it truly is, but I am actually a brother-in-Christ on *life* row. I have found eternal life here through my savior, Jesus Christ.

I just want to tell you how blessed I am by people like you. People you call *Christian* public servants. The *Christian* public servants around me, those who work here and volunteer here, look less at the outward appearance and, like our Lord, look more **at the heart**. Without excusing my past, they look less at what I did or my rebellious ways. They look less at my shame. Like the Lord, they look more at me as to *where I am* and *where I will someday be*.

Through His Word, and His people like you, my Lord has taught me to look at the heart of others. (You might think this is a lesson learned too late in my life, but still it is God's lesson to be learned.) So I am thankful for those who come to work and volunteer here. It's not an easy place to work or visit, I realize that. They have to be here because of me, and others like me. I know that. But they bless me each day. And I am blessed when I can bring our Lord to those around me, including a guard who may be having a terrible day or a free-world volunteer facing challenges of his own.

You are not thanked enough, but the world is blessed by people like you, *Christian* public servants. The world is truly blessed.

You may not work in a prison or volunteer on death row, but there are people around you who are *incarcerated* in some way – *incarcerated* by outward appearances. *Incarcerated* by temptation or by Satan. *Incarcerated* by fear or by shame. *Incarcerated* by the consequences of their own bad choices or godless actions.

Maybe it's the person working right next to you? I pray you will look at them less in terms of outward appearances and, like our Lord, look more at the heart.

Prayer: Father, in the name of Jesus, continue to mold my heart like Yours so I can meet brothers and sisters right where they are at. Amen.

— Jimmy Davis, Jr.

Each Friday, Jimmy and I joked, "Not bad for a kid with a 77 IQ!"

Expectations

The Parable of the Talents brings to light one death row man, Jimmy Davis, Jr. Recall in this parable, two servants performed righteously with what the master gave them to invest. A third servant was lazy and returned only what he was given. The master awarded more talents to those who invested righteously, and sent the lazy one "into the darkness, where there will be weeping and gnashing of teeth."

For thirty-four years of his life, Jimmy Davis, Jr. was the lazy servant or even worse. He was useless to God. He abused the talents God gave him, and he returned less than he was given. He followed this path during the first decade on death row.

Yet for the last 15 years, Jimmy focused on transitioning from the lazy servant into the best of servants who righteously invests God's talents. He says, "Now I use my influence to point people to Jesus." He transformed death row into Life Row. To him, Holman prison – including its barred doors – is now a fort that no longer incarcerates but gives protection to do God's work. This does not mean he wants to stay in prison, on death row or in the general population, but it does mean gaining comfort in a hellish nightmare.

Is Jimmy's investment current enough to wipe clean the slate from earlier years and avoid hell? Jimmy is prayerfully confident – more than I am about my own chances – of someday hearing the greeting, "Well done, good and faithful servant!" In the meantime, he writes, "If the Lord wasn't on my side, Holman prison would have overwhelmed and swallowed me up." Jimmy is certain he will not only avoid execution but also walk out of Holman prison into the free-world an innocent man. This is why, Jimmy argues, God has "given me more than 15 years of good, sound sleep."

I pray Jimmy is right. There are some death row men – even ones filled with faith in God – that I would shiver if they ever got out of prison. But Jimmy is not one of them. I would welcome him into my home as would anyone who has been touched by his God-given talents. So I praise God for putting him "in charge of many things."

The Jesus-Loves-Me paradigm underscores my prayer, and I believe God has forgiven Jimmy for all past sins, including the murder of Johnny Hazel – if he did it. But forgiveness, recall, is not a ticket into heaven. The Jesus-Means-Business paradigm requires I pray again – this time with *confident hope* that Jimmy is truly investing righteously his talents. From my cheap seat – partially obstructed by the world and my own humanity – I can only observe while God judges.

Let's review the moral lesson of this parable.

Expectation 1

Jimmy is expected to invest the talents God gives him.

Expectation 2

Jimmy is expected to invest God's talents *righteously*.

Assumption A

Jimmy's investments of God-given talent are to be *heightened* or *expanded*.

Assumption B

Jimmy must follow the *Holy Spirit* in investing his God-given talents.

Assumption C

Jimmy must invest in ways that *glorify God*.

Assessment

God gives talent, but for the most part, the world issues circumstance. What a difference Jimmy's free-world life might have been if a number of circumstances did not occur. A mother who brutalized him. A grandparent or great-grandparent who did not step in to stop the brutality. A loving father who died. The decision not to remain with a stepmom. An uncle who mentored street talents. A school system that did not diagnose a disability and, instead, processed a boy with "no value" until he dropped out. A defense counsel who did not check fingerprints on a gun, did not push the district attorney to pursue another man who might have committed the crime, and did not prepare Jimmy's mother on how to testify at sentencing. How tragic these circumstances were to his potential.

Yet circumstance does not forgive individual options. There are churches near Gurnee Avenue, and the great-grandmother was a faithful churchgoer. Jimmy could have gone to church with her and become involved with a church youth group. As a teenager, he could have sought help from a secular youth group located in Anniston, like the Boys and Girls Club of East Central Alabama. Millions grow up within the circumstance of poverty and some grow up in the circumstance of poor parenting. Relatively few turn to crime and murder.

Jimmy Davis, Jr. may not have entered the middle class, but he could have gotten a job, perhaps at the Direct Oil station. He might have been mentored by a nice man who smiled a lot, Johnny Hazel. Advocates of temperament theory argue God gives each individual unique mental attributes that can either be used for good or evil (Arno, 1994; Buss, 1975). Jimmy agrees. "We all have influence, good or bad, and it can affect people's lives forever."

In the free-world, the God-given talents of Jimmy Davis, Jr. were used lazily and abusively for trouble. The talent of leadership was used in the Gangsta Disciples. The talent of planning and acting were used to develop skills of stealing, escalating to skills of robbery, and culminating (remember, though, Jimmy claims he is innocent) with the skill of murder. The unrighteous use of talents continued when he arrived on death row.

It is through God's love – the Jesus-Loves-Me paradigm – that many find the way to see God as Lord – the Jesus-Means-Business paradigm. I pray this is the case with Jimmy Davis, Jr. He certainly found agape love at a weekend prison ministry. The home-baked cookies, as well as later deserts from food-prayers, brought more than a body of nourishment. Spiritual nourishment brought him a taste of agape love and a full helping of the Body of Christ. So did a man from New Jersey. So did his mentors in the Life Row Church. So did the parabolic professing of Jesus and the word of God. He has a remarkable talent to show agape love through listening, speaking, praying, and writing – all seemingly guided by the Holy Spirit toward the glorification of God. He's been exercising God's talents at increasingly heightened and expanded levels for nearly two decades on death row.

Is Jimmy Davis, Jr. investing God-given talents (Expectation 1)? Yes. Does he do so righteously (Expectation 2)? From my cheap seat, I believe so. Do his investments constantly heighten and expand his talents (Assumption A)? Amazingly so. Does he follow the Holy Spirit (Assumption B)? The Holy Spirit is present each time we interact. The same can be affirmed from many others who have Jimmy in their lives. Does he glorify God (Assumption C)? Yes, even when things are not going right. Even when the Miami Hurricanes lose a football game!

It wasn't easy for Jimmy to find reason or courage to use God's talents – righteously, ever reaching new horizons, guided by the Holy Spirit, and glorifying God. That's a tall order for anyone but especially for a death row man with seemingly nothing on either side of the barred door.

Yet God helped Jimmy win the struggle and find the courage to obey daily instructions. He received courage not to commit suicide. He found courage to be patient and to trust. Above all, he discovered courage to forgive. He has even forgiven his mother and understands her brutality was a function of being born to a drug-addict mother, the divorce from one husband and a death of another, and the stress of poverty. He tells me, "My mom carried a lot. Not just her kids, but her past, her failures… even her jobs. When she did whip me, it all came out on me." He is currently working on showing his mother the "God within me" and prays with confident hope she will return for a visit. He remains full of courage because "discouragement will blind me from the presence of Jesus and lead me to think of the worst outcome."

Postscript

I raised a question at the start of this chapter. Will the State of Alabama execute Jimmy? I hope not. But without God's intervention through the efforts of many people across the world, the State will most likely execute Jimmy Davis, Jr. Prison, especially death row, reminds us of life being a series of snapshots. In the State's eye, the snapshot of Davis-the-murderer automatically comes to the forefront. Even if the State sees the talents with which he has impacted people throughout the world, it is doubtful he will do anything but spend the rest of his life behind the barred door. Yet that would not be the "worst outcome."

I have written about a concept called *Justice of Misery Shared* (Slack, 2009). It is strange but very true: the only one who receives peace after an execution is the man being executed – if the death row man has found not only Jesus-Loves-Me but also Jesus-Means-Business. Everyone else, however, leaves the death chamber's witness rooms with as much pain and suffering as they had before the execution. This includes the victim's loved-ones. It is an agony that hopefully heals, but the scars are always excruciatingly present.

I argue the death row man should also wake up each day knowing about the suffering he has caused and he must bear. Justice of Misery Shared means there should be no difference between the victim's loved-ones and the murderer in terms of sadness and suffering felt each day for the rest of their natural lives. Justice of Misery Shared means the hellish state of mind for all remains as if there is nothing on either side of their respective emotional barred doors.

So it is my prayer that the State of Alabama grants Jimmy a change in punishment to life-without-the-possibility-of-parole. In a "law and order" culture like Alabama, life-without-parole is a feasible remedy – a just desert – for the murder of Johnny Hazel.

Until God Says I'm Ready

Hold on. Jimmy claims he is innocent. Hence, anything less than freedom is unjust. He has *confident hope* in God getting him out of Holman Prison. And so he waits on God.

Jimmy once told me a story about his great-grandmother canning preserves. He said, "This is what waiting on God is like."

> My great-grandmother canned a lot, and all the grandbabies loved her strawberry preserves. Behind her back we'd sneak a jar but could never open the lid. She'd take the jar and say, 'it's not time for this one. If we open the jar too soon, it will spoil.' She would take another jar of strawberry preserves and just tap twice on the lid for it to come off. She then smiled, 'Look! This one's ready. It won't spoil.' She knew when it was the right time for each jar.

The moral lesson, according to Jimmy, is *patience*. He writes,

> I am patient. I am the preserve in the jar. God is preserving me. If I open too soon, I will spoil. God is still preparing me for the day when He taps twice and the lid is sprung and I walk out of here prepared to obey His daily commands. So I sit and wait until God says I'm ready.

Will God continue to *preserve* his talents for the outside world? Or will God reward him into His world after execution? Jimmy believes the answer is "yes" to both questions. He once wrote,

> Trust is a word I hear used a lot, but people never fully get it. When you trust someone you are content with their decisions for you. Jesus was content to trust the Father all the way to the cross.

Jimmy trusts God and knows he will not spoil. God has given him talent as a gift that is weighted heavily by Jimmy's investment and acquisition of many coins of righteous acts. Yes, he abused God's talents and was once lazy and useless. However, today God, not just sleep, has taken away that constant nightmare he had since the first night on death row. Hell is no longer the *state of mind* of Jimmy Davis, Jr. – *on either side of the barred door.*

Chapter 4

Hell is a Gift Still Wrapped — No Steps to the Right

The Parable of the Sheep and the Goats

Why am I a death row man? Certainly not because of the time I spend there. Nor is it due to being a spiritual advisor to condemned men. I am a death row man for two reasons: (1) I have committed capital crimes against Christ and (2) Jesus is a death row man.

Like the chapters about Jack Trawick and Jimmy Davis, Jr., this one is about struggle with disobedience – a capital offence as told in the Parable of the Sheep and the Goats (Illustration 4.1). It is about *my* struggle. To place the struggles of Trawick and Davis into context, it was important to understand their respective backgrounds. So it is with my background. It was essential to seek intimacy and honesty about Jack and Jimmy. Therefore, the same level of truthful detail is afforded in this chapter.

In this parable, there are four key verses: (1) He will put the sheep on his right and the goats on his left. (2) Then he will say to those on his left, "Depart from me, you who are cursed, into the eternal fire prepared for the devil and his angels." (3) I was a stranger and you did not invite me in, I needed clothes and you did not clothe me, I was sick and in prison and you did not look after me. (4) He will reply, "Truly I tell you, whatever you did not do for one of the least of these, you did not do for me."

Illustration 4.1 The Parable of the Sheep
and the Goats Matthew 25:31-46

[31]"When the Son of Man comes in his glory, and all the angels with him, he will sit on his glorious throne. [32]All the nations will be gathered before him, and he will separate the people one from another as a shepherd separates the sheep from the goats. [33]He will put the sheep on his right and the goats on his left.

34 "Then the King will say to those on his right, 'Come, you who are blessed by my Father; take your inheritance, the kingdom prepared for you since the creation of the world. 35 For I was hungry and you gave me something to eat, I was thirsty and you gave me something to drink, I was a stranger and you invited me in, 36 I needed clothes and you clothed me, I was sick and you looked after me, I was in prison and you came to visit me.'

37 "Then the righteous will answer him, 'Lord, when did we see you hungry and feed you, or thirsty and give you something to drink? 38 When did we see you a stranger and invite you in, or needing clothes and clothe you? 39 When did we see you sick or in prison and go to visit you?'

40 "The King will reply, 'Truly I tell you, whatever you did for one of the least of these brothers and sisters of mine, you did for me.'

41 "Then he will say to those on his left, 'Depart from me, you who are cursed, into the eternal fire prepared for the devil and his angels. 42 For I was hungry and you gave me nothing to eat, I was thirsty and you gave me nothing to drink, 43 I was a stranger and you did not invite me in, I needed clothes and you did not clothe me, I was sick and in prison and you did not look after me.'

44 "They also will answer, 'Lord, when did we see you hungry or thirsty or a stranger or needing clothes or sick or in prison, and did not help you?'

45 "He will reply, 'Truly I tell you, whatever you did not do for one of the least of these, you did not do for me.'

46 "Then they will go away to eternal punishment, but the righteous to eternal life."

Jewish traditions permeate Jesus' parables. In the Sheep and the Goats parable, the Jewish notion of the right hand side means being on the side of justice (Levine and Brettler, 2017:57). His listeners understood that serving others meant serving God, and therefore, not helping those in need was actually a decision *not* to serve God (Levine and Brettler, 2017:58). When proclaiming the righteous will enter eternal life, Jesus knew the audience interpreted salvation as a function of works of compassion (Levine and Brettler, 2017:58). Hence, Jesus has three expectations concerning how we treat the least of His: (1) be on the side of justice, (2) serve God by taking care of others, (3) serve through works of compassion that help remedy injustice. Further God wants us to (A) expand works of compassion, (B) be guided by the Holy Spirit, and (C) glorify God (Morris, 1999; Turner, 2008).

The Moral Lesson

To avoid hell, seek justice through works of compassion. Do so wherever *He* calls you, including in *prisons*.

A Gift Still Wrapped – A Contemporary Parable

This is what hell is like. A servant of the Lord spoke about prison ministry to an adult Sunday school class. Placed next to the podium was a gigantic wrapped package. On it, so all could see, was an inmate's picture and the words, "Visit Me – Matthew 25:45." The servant posed a question, "If God gave you a gift, would you unwrap it?" Many viewed the big box as a ploy to get them to volunteer in prison ministry, and they replied accordingly. "No!" "I'm not called to prison ministry." "I'm called to do lots of things right here in our church." Several were honest: "I don't want anything to do with prisoners."

A few knew the meaning of Matthew 25:45 and responded, "Of course I will unwrap it. Give me the gift!" Each understood the many blessings received from opening *any* gift from God – blessings so great they would overflow even a box that huge.

That night a voice awoke the servant.

Despair not over those who choose not to visit Me in prison. They fear the steps to get to My right side. What they think is hell in this world is nothing compared to the place I will send them. Truly I say to those who keep my gifts wrapped, the comfort so desperately sought by rejecting Me will turn into the eternal fire.

The servant knew obeying God is not easy. Yet he realized, *hell is a gift still wrapped*. For those refusing that big box, there are *no steps to the right*.

Meet James D. Slack

About Calling

Some think what I do on death row is simply *my calling*, but not *their* calling. Yet each time that phrase is used, I wonder what God thinks. I mean, it's not *your* calling or *my* calling; it's *God's* calling.

Postmodernism domesticates that calling. Whatever is "enjoyable," that seems to be one's calling. Yet anything enjoyably done in God's name is a gift already unwrapped. The work is needed and guided by the Holy Spirit, but the gift's blessings make the work something akin to recess games on a *playground*. It is a time for meaning and fun while awaiting the bell to call you to another task.

When I hear the bell, always sooner than I desire, I know God requires me to get off the playground and out of my comfort zone. And as you will see, I struggle getting off that playground when He rings that damn bell!

Hence, prison ministry is not *my* calling. It is *God* calling me. Disobedience to His calling is a capital crime – according to Jesus, punishable by eternal death. My stay on death row is not a function of desire; it is a witness to His need. Comfortable? Not at first. Enjoy it? Only when the gift is completely unwrapped. Blessed by it? Yes, for two reasons. (1) It becomes a new playground when my comfort zone expands. (2) It is one further step toward His right side.

Born in Sandstone

I was born into a culture of sandstone. My birth occurred in 1952 in the college town of Oberlin, Ohio – about 30 miles west of Cleveland. This is where evangelist Charles Grandison Finney once preached, led the slavery abolition movement, and was President of Oberlin College. I grew up just north of Oberlin in the tiny (pop. 1,500) working-class village of South Amherst.

My great-grandfather was a common laborer in the "Duke's" sandstone quarry in Crich, Derbyshire, England. In the 1880s, he migrated with my great-grandmother and infant grandfather to South Amherst where new sandstone quarries were starting. By the 1960s, the village's sandstone quarry holes were the world's widest (over a quarter mile) and deepest (some around 800 feet). By that time, my grandfather and dad invested their lives in the quarries. For two summers, I swung a sledgehammer in a quarry hole. Each morning I climbed down a rickety wooden ladder (with lunch bucket tied around the neck) 300 feet to a wide shelf-edge still several hundred feet from the bottom.

Dysfunction

The all-white cross-road village was culturally isolated and infused with connotations of prejudice. The school system was the smallest and poorest in Northeast Ohio, and annually it earned the worst ratings in the state. Most kids became laborers in the sandstone quarries or workers in the nearby auto and steel industries.

My mother had an undiagnosed mental illness. I believe she loved me, but I cannot remember her telling me so. My older brother was detached yet manipulative. An older sister died at birth. I grew up knowing if Sally had lived, I never would have been conceived. By the time I was in the first grade, I started to pray each night to awake in the morning as an adult someplace else. That is what I prayed consistently until I left for college.

I was never physically abused by my mother, but I was hurt. So was my dad. Even on a good day, she was quirky.[1] Then there were other days. When I was in kindergarten, she perceived a temporary speech impediment (caused by a fixable dental issue) to be a sign I was gay. She was not one to hide her suspicions. (Unfortunately, this was the 1950s.) Despite my dad's objection, that year she dressed me for Halloween as a girl. From junior high through graduate school, she obsessed over my unintentionally dating only Roman Catholic women. Throughout the entire time growing up, with neither warning nor incitement, she would explode and rant for hours. When she became extremely irrational, my dad begged, "Just do as she wants or she'll end up in an insane asylum." Family behavior dictated not triggering her mood. This meant few conversations at home and even fewer while riding in the car.

Everyone tries to escape dysfunction. My dad escaped by voluntarily working long hours and choosing to take only five days of vacation per year.[2] My escape entailed Saturday bike rides to Oberlin where, just 6.4 miles down a country road, the New World began.

Oberlin was a treasure for a boy from seemingly another planet. In the 1960s, I watched with fascination Vietnam War protests and had fun imagining being a "hippie" Oberlin student. For a month or so one summer, I dated my first girlfriend of color. Her father worked at the Oberlin College Library. Within that library's hallowed walls, I learned about Finney and the social gospel. In high school, Oberlin College Library was where I studied. My parents knew about my sojourn, but the contents of that treasure were shared with no one. Oberlin was where I privately envisioned, planned and experimented with my future in a New World.

Reflection, not Blame

Reflection is different than blame. My mother's sickness was not her fault. Working class people, at least at that time, did not seek mental health care. Nevertheless on good days, she joined my dad in presenting a world

---

[1] She allowed no one wearing shoes – not even guests – to pass beyond the outside door because she feared soiling a spotless home. This rule applied even in the harsh northern Ohio winters. During summers, windows of our non-air-conditioned home remained unopened in fear of dust coming in.

[2] Because he worked so much, I frequently rode my bike to have lunch with him during summers. In the sandstone mill where he was foreman, not at home, we had wonderful conversations. After he died, I discovered he had accrued almost 400 days of unused vacation time.

outside the tiny village. Doing so, however, taxed their working-class pockets.

During the one-week annual vacation, we drove overnight (to avoid the cost of motels) to a cabin on Michigan's Grand Lake. On the way home, my parents whispered about having to cut back on eating meat for a couple of weeks to pay for the trip. Occasionally they drove my brother and me into other neighboring states – not to stop, but to turn around and say, "We've been there!" When I was in the 8th grade, my mother began working in a factory to save for my college education. During my sophomore and junior years in high school, my mom or dad (never together) drove me to visit many colleges in Ohio and the region.

I am certain my dad understood, but perhaps my mother did as well. My childhood prayer of waking up grown and heading someplace else had to be fulfilled. Despite family dysfunction and a culturally cramped village, my parents helped me build an exit ramp to get out.

The Duty of not Messing Up

The Slacks viewed themselves as one of several "blue blood" families in the village. My great-grandparents were part of a migration of Methodists and sandstone families from Crich. My aunt was on the school board and held state office in the teachers' union. My father was on the village council. Because of family status, I learned the duty of not messing up.

Around the 6th grade, I contemplated stealing a candy bar from the town's only gas station. While the owner was elsewhere, I stared enviously at a Milky Way chocolate bar. I almost grabbed it but, looking up at the last moment, I saw the owner watching me. I nervously smiled and walked away. He smiled and said, "You're a good boy!"

A Good Boy? Well, Not so Much

One Wednesday night, a couple of friends and I thought it would be fun to interrupt the worship service of what we called a "holy roller" church. It was fun until the pastor asked us to "testify." We quickly exited. In high school, my underaged friends and I routinely got drunk on Saturday nights at a Pizza Hut. We never paid the bill.[3] Driving home from college one weekend, I violated a stop sign in South Amherst. The village cop pulled

---

[3] One time I was so drunk I couldn't get up to use the restroom. I urinated under the table where my friends and I sat. They laughed but were also drunk enough not to realize their socks were soaked.

me over, and thank God, he was not terribly alert. My car was completely filled with pot smoke.

A Crime at Many Levels

One summer night before my high school sophomore year, I committed a real crime: trespassing, property theft, and animal cruelty. Most of all, it was a crime of breaking the heart of an elderly lady. She lived alone and always had a fat cat sitting on her lap on the front porch. Anyone walking by her home could see how much she loved that cat.

My friends and I saw the cat alone on the porch. We snatched it. At first we did it as a harmless prank, but things escalated. Someone challenged, "Hey, let's throw it down a quarry hole and see what happens." No one had the courage to disagree. So we took the cat to the edge of a large hole, figured out how to throw a cat without being clawed and dragged over with it, and then we drew straws to see who would do the tossing. All along, the cat fearfully meowed. After the toss, we listened as the cat whined and tumbled hundreds of feet until it fell onto the tall tree limbs near the bottom. Whine turned into screams. Quickly slamming onto the sandstone floor of the hole, scream turned into a prolonged agonizing moan.

Everyone got quiet. The suffering continued for what seemed an eternity. The cat finally relented to its fate, and we were immobile. Did we bargain for this fun? And what about that lady whom we all remembered as a nice cook in the school cafeteria? Each remained mute – imprisoned by conscience and perhaps captive of God's voice. Each wandered home alone.

We never boasted about the incident, nor talked amongst ourselves about the moral consequences. Frankly, we were fearful of being discovered. We never confessed to that lonely lady who had nothing in life but that fat cat. We didn't even think to buy her a kitten, ring the doorbell, and run like hell. But we saw her sitting on the front porch, calling for her cat, and looking so sad. She has certainly passed by now, but I am reminded of my complicity – and the pain I helped produce – whenever I return to the village and walk past her front porch.

Not a Practicing Christian

Until I was well into my 40s, I was not a practicing Christian. This was despite the efforts of my grandmother and aunt, both "good Methodists." While they practiced the Jesus-Loves-Me paradigm, neither neglected Jesus-Means-Business. As a preschooler, I followed a ball into the busy street in front of their home. I was oblivious to the screeching tires. One man pulled over and walked me to the front porch, rang the doorbell, and my aunt appeared. After the man left, she taught me about Jesus-Means-Business. Shaking her finger at me, "You must obey God, and you must obey His servants. And in this house, Jimmy, that means you must obey *me*!" She warned, "When I tell you to play in the back yard, do it!" There was no spanking, no withdrawal of love, no telling my parents. The punishment was her disapproval.

Also reflecting the Jesus-Means-Business paradigm were my grandmother's words after my father died. She asked me, "Do you think your dad's in heaven?" I told her, "Of course!" She hugged me and, without letting go, whispered, "Jimmy, I don't know for sure."

College

Both my grandmother and aunt were seed planters. But some seeds take time to root. This is especially true at college, where so many seeds land on rocks. When I came home my freshman year for Thanksgiving, I announced at my grandmother's table I was now an agnostic. I reported arrogantly what I "learned" about religion in my first philosophy course. Bless my grandmother and aunt! They tolerated my pseudo-intellectual rant, and before I returned to college, each reaffirmed their love for me. This time, both added, "God still loves *you*, Jimmy."

Four Initial Steps to Finding Christ

I was not looking for God, but seeds took root. My rebirth required four initial steps.

Step 1 – I married a Christian woman who both tolerated and changed me. She was a Southern Baptist but realized it would be easier to get me to God in a familiar faith setting – the Methodist church. She even let me believe it was my own idea to take that step!

Step 2 – I had a heart attack one Sunday after church. I developed a strange indigestion, but I assumed it was not a symptom. Eventually I drove to a hospital. Nothing was detected yet I passed out exiting the emergency room. I could have been killed driving home. The damage was small, but the event gave me pause as to why God spared my life.

Step 3 – During cardiac rehabilitation, I became aware of His intimacy. I learned to pray and, with each workout, my prayers increased in length. I wanted God to place His hand on my shoulder to guide and guard me. Eventually this prayer lasted almost two hours throughout my exercises.

One morning at the workout center, a mirror reflected my shirt with something around my right shoulder. It appeared to be blood. I quickly took off the shirt but found nothing. The stain was on the shirt's *outside*. It looked like a hand resting on my shoulder. That day, I became a believer in God.

Step 4 – The Holy Spirit entered my life. It happened when I was a pilgrim at an Emmaus weekend (Upper Room - Emmaus, 2020). The lay leader selected Jeremiah 29:11 as the guiding scripture for the weekend.

> For I know the plans I have for you, declares the Lord, plans to prosper you and not to harm you, plans to give you hope and a future.

On Friday evening, my future began. After dinner, as the evening activities were about to begin, I suddenly found myself dancing in front of everyone and singing "Jesus Loves the Little Children." Embarrassed, I apologized for my behavior. However, someone explained I was born again! Still a sinner, imperfect in this world, I became a practicing Christian. Jeremiah 29:11 remains my guiding Old Testament scripture.

The Plans I have For You

Everything in my life changed. For the first time as a professor, I realized I had not much to profess. Now I had Jesus to profess, and I boldly integrated His lessons into my work.

My writing transitioned from the sterile discipline-based analysis of the social sciences to a methodology I call theocentric phenomenology – incorporating His teachings in seeking the intimate reality of the human condition.[4] My "religion and politics" course no longer mocked faith but searched for its essence in our democracy. The ethics course turned toward the moral issues of life. The public policy course refocused on understanding the least of His. During finals week, I opened my office as a "safe place" for students to pray. I also prayed for individual students who were struggling in my courses.

Bad Things Happen

Like so many new Christians, bad things happened to me. The worst was this.

---

[4] Phenomenology is a philosophical methodology that looks at the *essence* of an entity. Unlike social science, it is not concerned with a relationship or cause and effect of variables. Edmund Husserl (2017) focused on the essence of encountering objects as they "are." Martin Heidegger (1962; 1968) and Hanna Arendt (2006) focused on the essence of human action, conflict, desire, oppression, and death. In this book, I examine the essence of action leading to hell.

Four days before Christmas, the dean summoned me to his office and gave me a choice: take early retirement or he would start the process of removing my tenure. I was then escorted off campus as a "danger" to students and faculty. Why? After mentoring a student having trouble passing my course, I said I would keep her in my prayers.

Good colleagues distanced themselves from me – most even denied my requests for support in finding another professorship. Several job interviews were rescinded because of a rumor I had "done something" to a student. (Yes, I had. My crime was prayer.) The shame of being escorted off campus, the damaging rumor, the collapse of career, and the immediate stress of not being able to say anything in the short-term out of fear of ruining Christmas for my family – all were unbearable. I contemplated suicide and had written my wife a letter.

Yet God had a Plan

Several pastors gathered and collectively laid hands on me for about four hours. They prayed, anointed me with oil, re-baptized me with water from the River Jordan, and then proclaimed God's plan for me did not include suicide. The letter to my wife became mute.

Slowly my reputation in the academy returned. Former students and colleagues offered letters of recommendation. I acquired a tenured full professorship at a Christian university. God called me to start *The Christian Public Servant*, which eventually was published as a series of books (Slack, et. al, 2015; Cooney, et al., 2017; Cooney, et al. 2018). He also gave me an opportunity to write a 2nd edition of a book about the essence of abortion and execution (Slack, 2014.). God persisted in renewing me, but He also persisted in His expectation that I visit him *regularly* on death row.

Getting off the Playground

When I was a child, it was always a struggle to get me off the playground. The same is true now. Regardless of how well God protects and blesses me, I am inclined toward *childish disobedience*. I just don't like hearing the bell ringing to end recess. However, in return for granting my prayer of adulthood (it took a little longer than one evening prayer!), God also required my obedience in His world. Despite my tremendous resistance, He showed me the steps toward His right. Here is an account of that struggle.

You Belong in Prison

Having been through Emmaus, *my* calling was volunteering on teams that conduct the wonderful weekend retreats. At one Emmaus training session, a friend said, "You belong in prison." I laughed, but he wasn't joking. He recited the tail end of Matthew 25:36, *I was in prison and you came to visit me.* "We don't visit inmates, we visit Jesus!" I still laughed and told him prison – even with Jesus in it – was not for me. He responded, "I didn't say it *was* for you. It's not for me, either. It's for *God*. You really want to serve God? Come with me to visit Jesus."

I was just fine with visiting Jesus at Emmaus weekends.[5] But did I just hear the bell ending recess? I hoped not! I was having too much fun doing the Lord's work where I was. I thanked my friend but re-affirmed my decision.

Six-months later, I saw my friend at another set of Emmaus training sessions. I heard, "Jim, *you* belong in *prison*." This time I smiled but did not laugh. "Look, I'll pray about it, but I don't think prison ministry is my calling." He corrected me, "It's no one's calling. You have no choice." He continued, "And besides, when someone starts a sentence with *I'll pray about it*, they're using prayer as an excuse for not serving God. Is that your plan, Jimbo?" Then he recited the tail end of Matthew 25:45, *whatever you do not do for one of the least of these, you did not do for me.* He concluded, "I just can't say no! Can *you*?" I remained, "This is not for me."

Yet now God had me thinking. The next day, I heard a shout, "Hey, Jim! YOU BELONG IN PRISON!" He recited the first part of Matthew 25:46, *Then they will go away to eternal punishment.* "You really want Jesus to send you to hell?" No, frankly, I did not. My friend kept pressing throughout the Emmaus weekend until finally, just to get him off my back, I said, "OK! I'll go just once!"

Belonging in Prison

At Donaldson Prison (near Birmingham, Alabama), I joined a Kairos ministry team that served the prison's general population (Kairos, 2020). It is a maximum security facility with the worst inmates in the state – murderers, rapists, gang lords, and drug dealers – who cannot behave in other prisons.

---

[5] While it was "my" calling, the Holy Spirit used Emmaus to build me up. I always came home a better husband, father, friend, person, and Christian. I grew addicted to the Holy Spirit who renewed me at each weekend retreat.

When I first entered the prison, I realized stereotypes aren't necessarily inaccurate. We passed through a pedestrian sally-gate, and the first thing I noticed was the razor-sharp barbed wire adorning the electrified fence. We walked down a gloomy and only partially lit hallway until we came to the first prison door. When it slammed shut behind us, I realized I was also imprisoned. So many thoughts ran through my mind. What if there is a riot? What if an inmate shanks me? And what is that smell? "Lord," I silently prayed, "do You really want me *here*?" Then another gate opened and slammed shut. Deeper inside the prison. Another gate. Still deeper. How would I get out in an emergency? My heart pounded.

We walked into the prison chapel and waited for the inmates – Kairos "pilgrims." I had to relieve myself, so I headed to the chapel bathroom. It had only one toilet and no urinals. My calculations indicated there would be over 75 inmates and free-world men in the chapel for four days. "And only *one* toilet?" Then an inmate dragged a waist-high rubber garbage container into the front of the bathroom. My heart rate skyrocketed knowing I was alone in a bathroom with an inmate probably serving a sentence of life-without-parole. "He has nothing to lose," I feared. But he apologized for the interruption, "You're new here. This is our piss-bucket for the weekend. The toilet is for sitting down. When the piss-bucket fills to the top, I'll need help emptying it. You assigned to be my helper?" Thankfully, I was not.

Each Kairos volunteer sponsors one pilgrim. My anxiety grew as I waited for mine. Then the inmates marched in, and Lord, what tattoos! Some arms were completely inked with the most awful inscriptions and pictures. Some had tears tattooed under their eyes – one tear for each person they claim to have killed *in prison*. Many had teeth missing, and again, what was that smell? The odor turned out to be the foulest collection of breath.

My sponsoree was just as uncomfortable as I, and this made it difficult to converse. We both asked questions only to receive monosyllabic responses. It was only the first night – Thursday – and Sunday seemed a lightyear away. My comfort zone leaked, and I longed to be back on a playground.

Yet God's hand remained on my right shoulder. I relaxed and my comfort zone gradually inflated. By Friday evening, the Holy Spirit had me hooked. By Saturday evening, I grabbed my friend and said, "You're right. I *do* belong in prison." I then *begged* to be included on future Kairos teams.

One More Step to the Right

It took a bit more time, but my comfort level increased to allow me to visit Jesus each week in Donaldson's general population – first in an accountability group and then as a course instructor in two faith dormitories. It still wasn't my calling: sweat dripping nonnegotiably during the humid and non-airconditioned summers; sitting on a toilet seat where cleanliness is not necessarily next to godliness; shaking hands with men who use their fingers to blow their noses. No, it wasn't *my* calling. It was *God's* calling. As much as I struggled, I knew I had to be obedient. At the end of each visit, He (not me) made it a bit more comfortable.

Then it happened again. A prison volunteer invited me to attend a bible study in Donaldson's satellite death row unit. Well, it was the same prolonged struggle to take another step. Every excuse came to mind and remained fixed for weeks. Because this was not *my* calling, I developed a terrible case of *lost ears*. However, God kept working on me. Thoughts of not visiting Jesus. Thoughts of not helping the least of His. Thoughts of going to hell. I kept going back to what I was told: *it's not about me; it's about God*.

So I ventured into that bible study group; and yes, I was afraid. To see general population men march into a room was one thing. To have men convicted of the worst crime sit on either side of me was inconceivable. But eventually I found my lost ears and listened to the death row men to my left and right. Stereotypes melted and mutual trust became a secure container for anxiety – much like that piss-bucket. I learned death row men are created Imago Dei despite murdering Imago Dei. God loves them no less than me. Conversations after bible study grew longer and, especially sports debates, became fun. God gave me another playground, this time shared by death row men.

Another Step toward His Right

Yet God continued to pull me from the playground. With similar struggle, He called me away from Donaldson Prison. A Kairos Ministry administrator requested I observe a death row weekend at Holman Prison.[6] My comfort zone was geared for a weekly one-hour bible study group at a small satellite death row unit – not a Kairos weekend event just yards from the execution chamber. So I told the administrator "I'd pray about it."

---

[6] Kairos Prison Ministry, International was not sure it wanted death row Kairos weekends because the format would not be identical to the general population weekends. My task was to assess consistency.

I tried to think of every excuse, but when I *actually* prayed, the Holy Spirit pounced on me. The bell was ending recess.

The entry hallways of Holman are painted in gulf pastels with slogans of encouragement on the walls. However, once back in the death row area, it was gloomy. The cells were much smaller than Donaldson's, and the dayroom for prison ministry activities was very tiny. This made the heat and humidity more pressing. And the men – Kairos pilgrims – were different on death row than in the general population – even different than the death row inmates at Donaldson. I guess Donaldson's larger cells and more accommodating dayroom could permit momentary forgetfulness about being on death row. At Holman, with the execution chamber so close and living spaces so cramped, it was impossible to pretend you were anywhere else.

All this has a bearing on the condition of the death row men. They are aged – many looking 20 years older than their birth certificates. Each has chalky skin from Vitamin D deficiency due to very limited access to sunlight. Each tried to smile, but everyone wished they were not here. Yet as before, by the second night, I begged the free-world volunteers to include me in subsequent weekends at Holman. This is how I met Jack Trawick.

Yet Another Step

Jack was arrogant and manipulative – the kind of inmate you want to avoid. Frankly, I left that weekend not giving any thought about him. For several years, my involvement with Holman death row men did not include Jack Trawick. Then God started to ring that bell! His voice interrupted my sleep: Jack Trawick is in need. Of course, I had *lost ears*. Yet He persisted. His instructions became clearer: God wanted me to write Jack Trawick a letter.

After several weeks, I promised God I would be obedient. I figured one letter was a short-term commitment. "Dear Jack, you may not remember me but I met you at a Kairos gathering a few years back. If you still have our group picture, I'm the guy with the aloha shirt. I hope you are doing well in this heat. Very best, Jim Slack."

DONE! God will certainly leave me alone for a while. By this time I had met Jimmy Davis, Jr. and others, and I felt comfortable with them. But I wouldn't feel comfortable with Jack Trawick. I did not know the particulars of his crime; it was just the way he acted at that Kairos gathering. For some reason, he seemed kind of creepy.

Well, God has a sense of humor. Just when I thought I was in the clear, Jack wrote back. DAMN! Now what do I do? God had a plan that included me responding each time Jack wrote me. Oh, I tried for weeks not to obey. But God was relentless. Again, I could not sleep because of His voice. So I wrote back, hoping Jack would go away. But he wrote back and soon we were exchanging three or four letters per week.

Jack eventually asked me to visit him during the execution week and to witness his death. As before, I struggled but finally agreed. About two months prior to his execution, Jack asked me to be his spiritual advisor. Now I was completely out of my comfort zone – to be responsible for helping prepare a man to meet God. I pleaded with God to reconsider His calling. But He did not. Ultimately I agreed to be obedient. Relying on His hand on my right shoulder, I prayed I would not mess up.

Capital Crimes Against Christ on Death Row

Success seems effortless to recall but failure is hard to forget. According to the Matthew 25 parables, failing to be obedient is a capital crime punishable by eternal death. Jesus states this explicitly in the Parable of the Sheep and the Goats. The disobedient on His left discovered too late the stakes were so high. Had they known, some might have had time to confess and rectify the verdict on their capital crimes. Hence, here I confess capital crimes against Christ on death row and pray my confession might bring reprieve.

Capital Crime of Lost Comfort

You might think lost comfort is something worthy of sympathy. Perhaps, but it is also a capital crime when the Lord depends on your comfort to do His work. In my experience on death row, losing my comfort zone does not occur every day, but when it happens it damages my ability to be obedient in serving God through the least of His. Here are four instances.

In a brief conversation, a death row man quickly slipped into graphic details of throwing his four children – ages about three, two, one, and four-months – off a high-rise bridge. He wanted to divorce his wife and avoid child-support. I believe he needed empathy for why he murdered his children. All I could think of were my children when they were toddlers. I really did not know what to say.

Another death row man asked for my "professional" help finding court cases that would *justify* his crime: drowning his wife in a bathtub so he could order a *second* catalog-bride. He wanted out of prison to finalize the purchase of the new wife. Even if he could get out, would there someday be a second bathtub drowning accompanying a third catalog wife? Again,

I did not know what to say, except "No. No, no, no, I am not your paralegal."

Still another death row man once asked, "Why do you hang out with the *enemy*." He meant members of the group called Victims of Crime and Leniency (VOCAL) – parents suffering because a child was murdered. When I explained they were also victims of the murder, he responded *"They just gotta get over it!"* I wondered why he didn't get it – he is the murderer and they are the victims. I shook my head but said nothing.

Through the cell bars, a fourth death row man suddenly switched the topic to his own case. He murdered an elderly woman who gave him a job on her Alabama farm. "The Mexican mafia was after me. I knew she worked for them. So I asked for a ride in her truck. I beat her up and threw her out and then drove to get my car." He rationalized, "I'm not the type to be cruel, so I went back with [my teenage son] to make sure she wasn't suffering. You know. She needed to be dead. But she wasn't. So I dragged her ass away from the road to some trees, put a big dead limb on her neck, and I stomped on that limb. Jim, I kept stomping so hard it hurt my hip! Really bad. So bad I had my son dig a hole to bury the bitch."

All this was said with steel eyes and without one glimpse of contrition. He looked as if to test me on how I would respond.

My God, how should I respond to all that? On so many levels, what he did was wrong. He murdered a kind elderly woman who gave him a job. He thought it more compassionate to complete the kill than to take her to a hospital. He bore no ethics about the complicity forced upon his teenage son. He felt sorry for himself because his hips hurt. And the Mexican mafia? What was *that* all about?

On that day, I really didn't know what to say about such insensitivity. As much as I tried, it caught me off guard. The death row man knew it too. Certainly, I would have been remiss if I focused only on the Jesus-Loves-Me paradigm. And clearly, he was not seeking a response concerning Jesus and hell. I wanted to walk away from this callous murderer and just go home. However, that would have completely denied Christ. So I just stood there and tried to smile. He won whatever game he was playing. In the process, I failed Christ.

A Capital Crime for Empowering a Junky

"Anthony" is a middle-aged Greek Orthodox man whose engineering firm transferred him from Detroit to Mobile – about 50 miles from Holman Prison. In Michigan, he was a prison ministry volunteer. Because

Michigan does not have capital punishment, its Department of Corrections maintains no death row. Perhaps this is why Anthony became involved with Holman's death row ministry. To be sure, Anthony is a brother-in-Christ. While he does many things for the glory of God, he has a tendency to transform into an execution junky.

An execution junky has several characteristics. First, he needs to be "there," believing the execution will be unsuccessful without him. Second, he tries to make friends late in the game – typically within a few months prior to the execution date. Third, he manipulates other death row men to solicit an invitation to be on the execution witness list. Fourth, he abuses the pronoun "I" and neglects the pronoun "He." Common red flag phrases are "I built these…" or "the men depend on me for…" or "I donate the money around here." An execution junky brags about what he did *to* the condemned man rather than glorifies God for what He did *for* the condemned man.

While Anthony does much good in death row ministry, it can become all about him. For instance, he insists on performing communion on execution days and boasts about how his Bishop (not his local priest) blesses the sacraments – as a special favor for him. So I knew things may go haywire when Jack Trawick informed me, about two months before his execution, that Anthony wanted to be placed on the execution witness list. I asked if he knew Anthony, and he said, "No. But 'Milkshake' [another death row man] vouches for him." I asked Jack, "What does Milkshake mean by 'vouching'?" He explained, "Milkshake says Anthony's a cool dude."

Well, it was Jack's execution week. If he wanted Anthony on his visitation list, I reasoned, that was his right. The point was to give Jack as much control over a situation that ultimately was not in his control. After placing Anthony on the list, as I suspected, Jack heard nothing from him for the remaining two months.

Recall from the Chapter 2, the execution week in Alabama runs from Monday morning to Thursday evening. Visitation on each day runs from 8 a.m. to 4 p.m. If there are no visitors, the condemned man must stay in his cell.

Monday at 8 a.m., I was in the visitation yard waiting for Jack. I was nervous. Could I keep a conversation going with him for eight straight hours? If no visitors showed, could I do that for four consecutive days?

When Jack entered the visitation yard, as described in Chapter 2, he was angry. However, I knew Jack liked to talk, especially about himself. The Holy Spirit led me to use this attribute to calm him down so eventually we could talk about God. So I just threw the ball up when moments of anger arose. "Jack, how does a car engine work?" "Jack, how do the lights work in this room?" "Jack, if you could invent a machine…?" Each question let him talk uninterrupted for hours. This permitted calm intermissions to talk about his last words, forgiveness, and his relationship with God. In those moments, it became clear he did not want many public displays of faith. He understood the importance of communion but, having received it once from the chaplain, did not feel it was needed for his last week in this world.

I followed the same strategy on Tuesday morning, and Jack remained calm to permit brief intermissions for further faith discussions. We also prayed in silence. Around 10 a.m., however, Jack got agitated. "Who's *that?*" I turned and saw Anthony being processed-in. I reminded Jack who it was, but his anxiety grew, "I don't know him." Anthony came in, yelling "Jack, so good to see you!" Anthony sat down, and Jack repeated he didn't know him. "Of course you do! I'm Milkshake's buddy. I saw you during visitation, remember? You're sitting over there, and I waved. Surely you remember." Well, Jack didn't remember. He got back to explaining how the lights worked, but Anthony interrupted to explain how he developed an innovative electrical system for a high-rise in Mobile. When I tried to calm Jack by getting back on the topic of the electricity in the visitation yard, Anthony chose to answer the question. This agitated Jack further, and Anthony seemed totally unaware.

Around 11 a.m., Anthony wanted me to leave the prison with him for lunch to "plan the rest of the week." Not being in control, Jack was nervous. Knowing he would have to go back to the cell if both of us left, I told Anthony I planned to eat from the vending machines with Jack. Anthony: "Why eat here? Vending machine sandwiches are crap. Hey, I know this restaurant…" He proceeded to talk about food Jack could never enjoy – and Jack was a glutton for food. Not convincing me to leave, Anthony left for lunch on his own.

After 4 p.m., when Jack left the visitation yard, I explained to Anthony my strategy for keeping Jack calm so that, during "intermissions," we could talk about God. I also emphasized Jack's feelings about public displays of faith. When Anthony brought up his expected role in communion, I clarified Jack's wishes would be followed, and as of today, he did not want communion. Anthony strongly objected, reminding me he had been to "a lot" of executions and "that's just not the way it's done."

Jack's cousins arrived at 8 a.m. on Wednesday. It was a family reunion, and I considered my role to be secondary. I took a seat away from Jack so the family was center at the table. When Anthony arrived, he sat with me but was clearly dissatisfied. One cousin inquired, "You look lonely. Come join us." Anthony quickly moved to the center of Jack's family and began to monopolize the conversation. Jack grew increasingly anxious.

On Thursday afternoon, just a couple of hours before the execution, I left the visitation yard for a moment. I needed to pray alone. It was my first (and I prayed the last) execution to witness. When I returned, Anthony had already completed communion – despite Jack's wishes! Everyone was still in a communion line and all looked upset. Jack whispered, "He forced communion." I started to say something to Anthony, but Jack's matriarch cousin whispered, "Let's just move on."

About an hour before Jack went back to the death cell for the final time, a CO offered to take polaroid pictures. I wondered why anyone would want a picture taken at this point. To my shock, each cousin wanted a picture with Jack. To my horror, Jack wanted a picture with *me*. Posing with him, Anthony suddenly stood, "I'd like to be in the picture." Jack looked at me and slightly shook his head indicating "Let's get this over with too." Jack quickly handed me the developed polaroid picture and said, "Promise me *you'll* be the one to keep it."

The bottom line is this: I poorly handled the situation with the execution junky. I should have protected Jack better, and that should have started with me being honest about placing an execution junky on the visitation list. I let Anthony exploit Jack, his family, and even his lawyer – all pressured to take a communion none wanted – especially the lawyer, whose faith is Judaism. I was afraid a confrontation between Anthony and me would harm Jack's mental state and thereby make it harder to prepare him for the Foot of the Throne as well as lodge greater burden on the execution team in performing its responsibility. In not finding a way to shield Jack and not finding a way to form a team with Anthony, I failed Christ.

Postscript on the Junky

Recall the contemporary parable, *A Gift Still Wrapped*. Its point was: obeying God is not easy. What if Anthony was right? Was his self-absorption only the wrapping paper on a box I refused to open? Was I interfering with God's plan for Jack, Anthony, and me? Perhaps Anthony was right about the need for communion prior to Jack's execution. It was the first time I was a spiritual advisor, and Anthony had much more experience. Did my ego get in the way of God? I really do not know if I helped Jack by keeping him calm or if I hindered his preparedness at the Foot of the Throne by not permitting Anthony to do God's work. The servant in the contemporary parable was right. Obeying God is not easy. Either way I stepped, it might well have been an act of disobedience with the stakes so high.

A Dream Capital Crime

Jimmy Davis, Jr. is "married" to Susan.[7] They dated prior to Jimmy's conviction, and at that point, Susan's life went forward. She has two sons and several grandchildren.

About ten years ago, they renewed their relationship. A few years ago, Jimmy asked if I would drive her to Holman for visitations.[8] While Susan and I have enjoyable conversations on those drives, one of her stories lingers. She claims God has given her the talent of dreams. One of her dreams involves Jimmy, his lawyer, and me. We are standing outside the front entrance of Holman prison and Jimmy is a free man.

Susan has Jimmy convinced he will not be executed. This makes Jimmy's spiritual preparation much more difficult. Susan is planning to attend his execution week and that dream makes preparing *her* practically impossible.

I've talked with her about the power of prayer and the control God has over Jimmy's life. I have tried to remind her that God's answer to prayer about Jimmy might not be what either of us desire. Because of this, I explained, there is a need to be ready for the most likely outcome – execution. She refuses to give it any consideration and intends to hold onto her dream even after Jimmy is strapped on the gurney. "A miracle will happen! I'll keep shouting that," she repeats, "so he won't have to close his eyes." Jimmy is convinced her dream holds truth.

Fact is, no death row man walks out the prison front door with his lawyer and spiritual advisor. The best that can happen is another trial or a change in Jimmy's sentence to life-without-the-possibility-of-parole. Not being able to prepare Jimmy or Susan for the reality of the worst-case scenario (execution) or the limitations of the optimal scenario (life without parole) is another sign of failing Christ. Unlike many already fixed on the left side of Christ, it is a capital crime I still have time to rectify. I

---

[7] They are "married" but no paperwork has been filed. They married each other over the phone. In the past, Alabama death row marriage ceremonies were handled just like those in general population: either the chaplain or a free-world pastor would marry the couple in the visitation yard. Since the passage of AR 407, a death row man only needs to complete DOC paperwork and send it to the fiancé who submits it to a judge where she lives. No pastor or chaplain is now involved in the marriage process. Alabama permits no conjugal visits.

[8] I was blessed to do so, but it turned a round-trip ride from seven hours to well over ten hours.

must find a way to get Jimmy and Susan to place the dream into the perspective of prayer and understand God may have a different answer to that prayer.

Postscript on the Dream

Recall once again the contemporary parable, *A Gift Still Wrapped*. What if Susan is right? What if her dream is a gift I am unwilling to unwrap? I could fail Him in affirming the dream or denying its validity – either way committing a crime against Christ. Yes, obeying God is not easy. There really are no easy steps to His right.

Expectations

In the Parable of the Sheep and the Goats, Jesus professes this moral lesson. Seek justice for the least of His by serving God through works of compassion wherever He calls you, including prison.

We can assume everybody facing Jesus believes they are Christians since each one calls Him, "Lord." However, many are wrong. He quickly divides the room. On his right, the side of justice, He places the obedient. Everyone else – the disobedient and the insufficiently obedient – go to the left. Deficient to His expectations, the group on the left did not serve Him through works of compassion for the least of His. They committed capital crimes against Christ because they neglected His calling. On too many occasions, they did not invite the stranger in, clothe the poor, look after the sick and the imprisoned. They probably did some of this, in selected situations within their comfort zones, but failed to realize His expectations are neither a "check list" nor a "pick and choose." They focused on their own calling and, therefore, were sentenced to eternal fire.

You now know my struggle to try to end up on His right. For two decades, that struggle to obey His calling has directed me toward prison and then death row. Despite my sins, God rescued me on so many occasions. However, I prefer the playground and do not like when recess is over. In times of trouble, I confess I rely on the Jesus-Loves-Me paradigm. In good times, my confession remains the same. Certainly, the spiritual seeds planted by a grandmother and aunt were life-rescuing, as necessary as the four initial steps leading me to practicing Christianity.

Yet more than initial steps are required to finish on His right side. The Jesus-Means-Business paradigm hangs over my head at every moment in my life. I am never sure how many steps are needed, and I do not know when time will be up.

According to the parable's moral lesson, I must:

Expectation 1

Be on the side of justice for the least of His.

Expectation 2

Serve God by taking care of the least of His.

Expectation 3

Take care of the least of His through works of compassion.

Assumption A

Expand His works of compassion.

Assumption B

Follow the Holy Spirit in performing each work of compassion.

Assumption C

Glorify God in all works of compassion.

Assessment

It is easier to detail your actions than to self-assess your performance. Because the stakes are highest when it comes to complying with the Lord's expectations, it is especially hard to self-evaluate. Before venturing into appraisal, I need to raise three issues.

(1) Who is the Least of His?

Matthew 25:31-46 does not offer a comprehensive list of "the least of His." Certainly, everyone fits into the "least of His" category – born and unborn; female and male; rich and poor; red, yellow, black, white, and brown – from conception to grave. Yet if Jesus stressed every individual was "the least," including me, I would be off the hook. I could simply tap postmodernism to domesticate His expectations and answer Him in reconstructed obedience. "I'm taking care of myself, thank you very much." Or "I'm doing enough already with my family, can't you see?" Even when He awakes me at night, I could say "I don't need to do anything outside of my church. Now go away and let me sleep!"

Like you, I have loved-ones and friends in need of compassionate works, some in dire need of justice. God does not want them to be ignored.

However, the thrust of this Matthew 25 lesson is to stretch my comfort zone and take care of Him where He is a stranger needing compassionate works leading toward just remedies. I simply must go where I don't want to go.

(2) Funny Thing about Works of Compassion

Some actions appear easier than others. Taking canned goods to a church food pantry is less of a task than feeding a poor man at my home. Giving a bottle of water to a homeless woman on a street corner is less of a stretch than driving her to a supermarket and paying for what she needs. Donating to a homeless shelter seems more reasonable than letting a homeless family live in my basement. It is more bearable visiting an adult neighbor in hospice than taking time to play with a neighbor's toddler who lies terminal in a pediatric cancer ward. The Jesus-Loves-Me paradigm – by itself – tempts postmodern domestication to cater comfortability.

(3) Justice of His Love

Perhaps the most uncomfortable situation deals with a condemned man or woman. Discomfort comes not from the condemned being terminal. It is because the condemned has caused so much death and consequential agony.

Yet Jesus expects me to take care of the least of His – in this case, death row men – because each death row man is actually *Him*. I must respond *intimately* to these least of His and try to figure out some kind of remedy for justice. If limited to worldly definition, His justice may never be found in my (or anyone's) heart and mind. However, no one is limited to this-world explanation. Therefore, I confess *the justice Jesus advocates is the untiring justice of His love*. It is agape love that must be shared with all, not just the comfortably selected.

This is the core of the Jesus-Means-Business paradigm: obediently disengage the "me" in the Jesus-Loves-Me paradigm – *not for my sake (nor your sake) but for the sake of taking care* of the least of His. Then await for His judgement on my acts.

Now, What's the Assessment

Am I seeking justice (Expectation 1)? Yes, but what is the justice of His love for the man who wants nothing more than another catalog bride? Is the justice of His love found in not convincing a man the spiritual utility of communion before he is executed?

Am I serving God by taking care of others (Expectation 2)? I try but too often my service gets blemished by my inability to shower agape love over a man who killed his children or another man who cannot understand the pain his murder brings to victims still surviving.

Am I performing works of compassion (Expectation 3)? Insufficiently. Works of compassion can be thwarted easily by my intolerance toward a brother-in-Christ who seems ill-fit for execution ministry, as well as my inability to build a team with him that glorifies God. Works of compassion become tainted by my frustration with someone who proclaims God's power in her dream.

Are my works of compassion expanding (Assumption A)? Yes, but it seems I never return to previous worksites (those old playgrounds) to continue my obedience there. Hence, I do not fail in moving sequentially, but I fail expanding architectonically – the house He is building in my heart ends up having no other floors than the one I am currently on.

Am I following the Holy Spirit (Assumption B)? Yes, but many times reluctantly. God has to drag me kicking and screaming from any play ground.

Am I glorifying God (Assumption C)? I try but, perhaps more than Anthony, the "I" in me comes out more than the "He." (How frequent have you read the pronoun "I" in this chapter?) My ego is difficult to control.

No Excuses

I highlight my failures, not His successes, because the Parable of the Sheep and the Goats affirms failures count dreadfully. I have no excuses for my childish disobedience. My blessings were more than sufficient. I did not have to worry about gangs when I rode my bike, nor did I worry about the bike being stolen when left outside. Family dysfunction and small-town myopia were stifling but ordinary: the stuff endured by millions of others. My parents allowed me respite in Oberlin and, by their sweat and hard-earned wages, built me a one-way exit ramp into college and away from village and family. I was fortunate to have a grandmother and aunt who taught Jesus-Loves-Me and showed Jesus-Means-Business. I was blessed to find a good wife, a necessary heart-attack, a prayer in rehab, and the Holy Spirit on a Friday night. In essence, there is nothing in my background that would drive me away from obeying His expectations.

In too many instances, far beyond what I detailed, I embraced my calling over His calling.

The Bell Ringing

Jesus never invites me to choose works of compassion that fit *my* comfort zone over the horribly distasteful and odorous corners of His need. Yet I should be grateful to hear that bell ending recess. After all, it signals He has not given up on *me*. He still expects me to be "there" *for* Him and *with* Him where works of compassion are needed to address injustice. This is why He prevents me from sleeping the sleep of the innocent. I am not a murderer awaiting execution in Holman's death chamber, but I am not innocent of *capital crimes against Christ*. He awakes me because of my guilt.

Unanswerable Questions

Did I truly help Jack Trawick? Am I actually serving Christ through Jimmy Davis, Jr.? And what about the others with whom I interact because of death row: COs, the chaplain, other death row men, and the few loved-ones death row men find waiting with me in the visitation yard? Only God knows the ratio between my failures and His success. Only He knows the time I have to alter the equation.

Postscript on James D. Slack

No further steps will be afforded if I avoid unwrapping His gifts. And I know the greatest gift is the hardest to open: spreading the justice of Jesus' love – *not for my sake but for the sake of the least of His*. With His hand on my right shoulder, I must quickly unwrap and obediently listen for His next calling and His final judgement.

I must understand there are no easy steps to the right.

Chapter 5

Closer to an Innocent's Sleep – Murder's Noise

Murder's Noise

We are reminded "noise can blight our soundscape as surely as pollution and trash cans scar our landscape" (Webb, 2011:30). While fingers in your ears may block soundscape noise and hands over your eyes can blind landscape scars, no part of your body prevents the damage caused by noise to your *spiritscape*. Here, I speak of *murder's noise* that comes from capital crimes against Christ and the fear of a verdict that sends you to hell. It is a noise that settles in your soul and is hard to dislodge.

Murder's noise robbed Macbeth of the "innocent sleep that soothes away all our worries. Sleep that puts each day to rest. Sleep that relieves the weary laborer and heals hurt minds." This is why Macbeth shrieks, "I thought I heard a voice cry, 'Sleep no more! Macbeth is murdering sleep'" (Shakespeare, 2013). For those who murder Imago Dei or murder obedience to God – that is, everyone living on their own death row and subject to eternal damnation – murder's noise removes the possibility of sleeping the sleep of the innocent.

Murder's Noise – A Contemporary Parable

This is what hell is like. There was a woman named Pony who served the Lord with all her heart. Then her only son, Michael, was murdered on Mother's Day eve. Nothing was the same, and she drifted from God. Days were expended before the sun rose. Holidays were emotionally vacant. Even answering the phone was unbearable for its ring once reported Michael's death. Pony was hostage to murder's noise: empty noise without Michael; untruthful noise causing doubt about each remembered *I love you*; silent noise of Michael dying amidst screams of his fiancé; soundless noise of grandchildren never-to-be-born by Michael; self-imposed noise of Pony's perceived inability to save her only son; gossip noise of friends whispering, "Pony needs to *just get over it*." Murder's noise prevented an innocent's sleep.

Then one night she heard a voice:

> My sweet daughter, I shower you each day with My love. Don't you feel it? I truly hear your murder's noise for I also lost My only Son to murder. And too many keep murdering Him with their disobedience to Me. Know this: I will judge Michael's murderer but that is My business, not yours. Know this too: your business is to return as my obedient servant. In my name, I want you to do good deeds, act righteously, and seek My justice in works of compassion – not to those familiar to you but to men like Michael's murderer. Yes, I send you to comfort men beyond your comfort – men who murder My Image. Remember, My justice is the justice of My Son's love shared infinitely with all. I promise, murder's noise will subside and your hell will abate. Through obedience to Me, you will relearn how to sleep the sleep of the innocent.

Pony's talent is baking. She acts righteously (morally and honorably) in seeking His justice – the justice of Jesus' love – by sharing her best brownies with Holman's death row men. She knows Jesus is a death row man, and through the brownies, she visit's Him. Because of her work of compassion, the brownies are devoured lovingly by the least of His. Yet her good deed also lets death row men devour Michael's story, told each time the brownies are shared on Kairos weekends. They cry openly. Death row men, too, hear murder's noise and seek the same innocent's sleep.

Relearning how to sleep the sleep of the innocent is not an easy task. Yet Pony and Holman's death row men have learned by sharing His love, murder's noise recedes and this-world's hell mollifies a blessed bit.

Matthew 25 parables

The Matthew 25 parables are about the commission of capital crimes against Christ. By failing to meet God's expectations, you and I subject ourselves to a judgment of eternal damnation – becoming dead to heaven – the ultimate penalty in a spiritual capital crime.

Murder's noise helps disrupt the spiritscape by blocking the meaning of "Gospel," or Good News.[1] It thereby invites rationalization created by postmodernism. We end up mistakenly assuming the Good News means

---

[1] The word, gospel, is derived from the Greek word Euangelion. The prefix "eu" means good and "angelion" means message. Together, this word presents the Good News of imputation – the transfer of our sins to Christ on the cross and the transfer of His righteousness (morality, truthfulness) to the believer.

no further action is ever required. That is, somehow His love, forgiveness, and grace comprise the final step for entry into heaven. This is how the Jesus-Loves-Me paradigm trumps the Jesus-Means-Business paradigm. You and I – along with all other death row people including Jack Trawick and Jimmy Davis, Jr. – cannot hear the Gospel and, thereby, become convinced we can transform its message into a pass for avoiding hell. Yet, as argued in Chapter 1, Jesus' love does not guarantee anything but a *first step* toward heaven.

Such confusion may be why – even before the advent of postmodern thought – Jesus felt the need to cut through murder's noise with crystal clear moral lessons from three parables. In the Parable of the Ten Virgins, Jesus uses the metaphor of the banquet hall and the symbolism of the locked door to explain the death penalty. The Bridegroom simply states, "I don't know you," and this is akin to how the guilty is strapped onto an execution gurney. Yet many people today, like in Jesus' day, do not grasp the moral lesson of His death penalty.

Jesus escalates his lesson in the Parable of the Talents. The lazy servant is not only stripped of gains, the Master deems him "worthless" and throws him "into the darkness where there will be weeping and gnashing of teeth." Unlike the five foolish virgins, the lazy servant can't even press his nose against the door in an effort to gain sympathy. His execution happens alone and out of sight. Yet people still don't "get it" – not in Jesus' day nor in ours.

Therefore, Jesus escalates the moral lesson to the clearest summit via the Parable of the Sheep and the Goats. Without metaphors, He personally culls His followers. The ones on the left do not meet His standard in serving the least of His and, hence, have not done enough for Him. He sends them into eternal punishment. And like in the day of Jesus, we don't get it.

You may ask, how much is enough to meet His measure? Jack Trawick pondered this question. Jimmy Davis, Jr. and I worry about an answer. The fact is, only He knows the measure and time and that gives urgency to do more good deeds, continue acts of righteousness, and always seek the justice of Jesus' love through works of compassion. Until Judgement, we will not know when and if enough is enough!

Three Death Row Men

Jack Trawick, Jimmy Davis, Jr. and I are products of very different backgrounds. Jack Trawick came from a life of privilege. He had access to the best healthcare systems, great schools, and even greater opportunities. Jimmy Davis, Jr. grew up in poverty without hope. Gurnee Avenue provided little opportunity other than learning the skills of street survival. I grew up somewhere in between Jack and Jimmy – a rural working-class village with some poverty and a hefty dose of marginalized opportunity.

Just about everyone in Jack's community went to college – some went to the world's finest institutions. Jimmy knows no one who went to college. There were 38 students in my graduating class. Only three went directly into college – and some did later in life. The three attended good state universities but only two graduated. A few more became nurses and technicians, but so many were tossed a life with only small-town options.

Jack, Jimmy, and I came from different kinds of dysfunction. For instance, Jack's family knew the value of higher education but used it as a placebo of hope that college life would somehow dispel Jack's burgeoning drive for rape, torture, and murder. Jimmy's family did not know the value of college, and even if it did, the price tag was well beyond imagination. Having never been to college, my parents speculated on the potential of its value but, whatever the actual worth, assumed a university education was a necessity for a son wanting out.

Despite dysfunction, one commonality was the absence of murder in the respective families. Jack's dad may have been too busy at work, but he did nothing to foster Jack's abnormalities. Jimmy's mother was too busy beating him and left the lessons of the street to his uncle. While Jimmy's uncle taught him how to lie and steal, he did not teach him murder. My dad worked long hours for escape but built a bond of love and support through lunchtime talks and time spent driving to and from prospective colleges. Murder was not taught.

What if background settings were switched? Would Jack still become *that monster*? Most likely. Within any setting and family, limiting that monster – with no professional assistance – would have been impossible. His best shot at normality was through his own affluent family, not families of lesser means in Anniston, Alabama or South Amherst, Ohio.

What if I had exchanged places with Jimmy? Would I have become a gang member on Gurnee Avenue to get away from an abusive mother? Yes, but I would have been killed on the streets. Although there were alternatives in Anniston, it appears family members had no capacity to make connection with those institutions, and therefore, the only link was to the street.

Would Jimmy have gained from trading places with me in South Amherst? I hope so. With a caring father, he could have conjured a future by travelling on a country road to Oberlin. He would have benefited greatly from a grandmother and aunt who planted seeds about God. I suspect those seeds would have blossomed sooner in Jimmy than the time they took to root in me.

Here is what I see: My disobedience probably started with fantasizing about a Milky Way chocolate bar at Makruski's Garage and continued with a car full of pot smoke. And yes, in between, there was that cat. More importantly, my disobedience is *on-going* each day I awake. What I described is true, but those events are far from being inclusive and exhaustive of my life.

Jack's background should have led him to mental health accommodations and, if so, perhaps a bright future in his dad's engineering firm. However, that did not happen. Jack's path to death row became predictable, starting with His disobedience regarding sexual improprieties proffered to his sister.

In Jimmy's case, there was nothing about stealing puppies and bicycles that automatically brought into play a convenience store murder. Tragically Jimmy's story may not even be about disobedience leading to murder. His background could easily have led an innocent young black man to a painfully wrong guilty verdict and death row. This is what Jimmy Davis, Jr. claims, and he is who I believe.

Please understand, no one's background proves ill-suited to the Gospels – especially the obedience professed by Jesus in the Matthew 25 parables. For Jack to find God's obedience, he required control mechanisms of healthcare and family. These simply did not function. Jimmy learned about God's obedience after a decade of dying on death row. I am convinced Jimmy's obedience to God will remain constant regardless of whether Susan's dream is realized, or he is resentenced to life-without-parole in general population, or even if he is strapped to a gurney in the execution chamber. I am certain Jimmy's obedience will remain sound while God and the State of Alabama sort out his future.

As for me, I will continue to struggle. I realize God has me on another playground – death row – and I have been here for more than 20 years. I fully expect to hear that bell ring. I do not know where He will lead me. I pray He will relieve me from further executions and reward me with a most comfortable assignment: tending full-time to my beloved grandchildren. (I suspect He will give me that blessing coupled with another challenging assignment and help me with both.) Nevertheless, I acknowledge that bell will mark God's calling, not mine. For Jimmy and me, obedience to God will certainly bring each of us *closer to an innocent's sleep*.

Your Capital Crime Against Christ

The first chapter ended with introducing the idea of *capital crimes against Christ*. This chapter concludes by raising the issue again. This time, however, the focus is on *your* capital crimes against Christ.

Now, this is the point when murder's noise triggers postmodernism enabling you to domesticate this issue. You might think, "I know Jesus is a death row man, but He's also a poor man and a sick man. Come to think of it, He's also a hungry man, a man without clothing, and a man who needs comforting. Wait a minute! He's also a female and a child and a senior citizen. Oh no, Jesus is also a different color and race than me." And you probably forgot Jesus is a communist, a Nazi, a Muslim, a Jew, a Hindu, a Buddhist, another religion, an atheist, and someone who is lesbian, gay, bi-sexual, transgender or queer (LGBTQ). Jesus is also that little girl who needs math tutoring and the lonely lady down the street with a cat.

Now you must feel overwhelmed, maybe frightened, and perhaps way out of your comfort zone. So it is easy to domesticate the multifaceted Jesus and rationalize, "I can't care for Him *everywhere*." Or "I don't want to care for him *there*!" You might decide either to serve Him within the limits of your comfort zone or not serve Him at all. Resist these temptations.

Remember, *postmodernism* is our society's elixir to deconstruct and reconstruct truth and reality to fit our own needs. On many issues, doing so is sort of harmless. (If you're like me, you drive down a particular street so you can rationalize violating your diet for an ice cream sandwich or a couple of donuts.) However, a crime against Christ is committed when you use postmodernism to rationalize disobeying the moral lessons found in the bible, especially (for our purposes) those found in the Matthew 25 parables. Its alchemy disputes you have absolutely no choice but to meet God's expectations about obedience. You don't have to be a brain surgeon or theologian to understand completely the great fallacy of our culture: echoing the self-vindicating "good" news about love (the *Jesus-Loves-Me paradigm*) is more important than hearing the "necessary" news of "how to avoid hell" (the *Jesus-Means-Business paradigm*).

In addition, you may try to domesticate other scriptures to the point where you can hum the hymn "Jesus Loves Me" and imagine loving you is the only kind of love Jesus has. But that's not true. While He lovingly transfers your sins to Him and His morality (righteousness) to you, the question becomes: What do you do next?

The answer is this: He expects you to share His love with others through good deeds, righteous acts, and justice through works of compassion. The answer is anchored to His calling, not your preference. Preference makes room for domestication. Domestication leads to disobedience. Disobedience is a capital crime against Christ. A capital crime against Christ makes you subject to His judgement on a death penalty in hell.

Your claim of having *lost ears* will not stop murder's noise. No, murder's noise will still get in the way of understanding the quiet intimacy of His love toward others – even strangers in dire need. The Jesus-Means-Business paradigm begs to find your lost ears, clear your murder's noise, and recognize your spiritscape – *His calling* – to spread His love. His call requires confession that you will be judged on the basis of doing what He needs and when He needs it done. After all, it was not the five Foolish virgins who made the rules; neither were the rules made by the lazy servant nor those on the left. It is God who sets the rules and makes the calling – again, His calling, not yours. His love is not your tool for self-embellishment; rather, *you* are His tool for showering His love onto the suffering of others.

Do you feel stressed out? Me too. After all, I have done little more than visit Jesus on death row for the last 20 years. Am I missing His call? Maybe. I have not been to a hospital unless it was to visit a family member. In the last ten years, I have fed very few of the hungry and have clothed even fewer of the needy.

Jesus' call changes when He needs you someplace else. Usually His call will entail expanding the comfort zone. When our respective comfort zones become threatened, perhaps you and I can learn from Jimmy Davis, Jr. This servant of the Lord, coping with *borderline intellectual disability*, wrote:

> I am never comfortable so I'm always pushing myself. At the start of this year, I went in prayer and told Jesus I don't want to give His people what I used to give them. I want to make a spiritual impact in their lives. A spiritual impact where they experience Him and not me. Whatever they are going through, they hear His voice and not mine. I want to launch deeper in my relationship with Him. Launch deeper in spending time with Him. Launch deeper in reading and studying His word. Launch deeper in my relationship with the Holy Spirit. Most importantly, I want to launch deeper in obeying Him. *It is fruitless to ask Jesus to help me if I don't obey Him.*

Forget the comfort zone. It will do no good to ask for Jesus' help on Judgement Day when disobeying Him today. Let God launch *you – where* He needs you and *how* He needs you. Be obedient to His business, and His business alone.

I hope Jack Trawick met Christ's measure. I pray Jimmy Davis, Jr. will do the same. As for me, I ask for your prayers in my continued struggle.

For you, I pray you will hear and obey His calling, ignore your comfort zone, and dislodge from your soul the murder's noise.

I pray you will draw closer to an innocent's sleep.

References

AL.Com, 2009. "OUR VIEW: Alabama Shouldn't Even Execute Serial Killer Jack Trawick." June 11. https://www.al.com/birmingham-news-commentary/2009/06/our_view_alabama_shouldnt_even.html. Retrieved April 4, 2020.

Anniston, Alabama. 2020. http://www.annistonal.gov/. Retrieved 6.7.202.

Arendt, Hannah. 2006. *On Revolution.* New York: Penguin Classics.

Arndt, W., Danker, F. W., & Bauer, W. (2000). *A Greek-English lexicon of the New Testament and other early Christian literature* (3rd ed.) Chicago: University of Chicago Press.

Arno, Richard G. 1994. *Temperament Theory.* Sarasota, Fl: National Christian Counseling Association.

Atkins v. Virginia (00-8452) 536 U.S. 304 (2002) 260 Va. 375, 534 S. E. 2d 312, reversed and remanded.

Bainton, Roland H. 2013. *Here I Stand: A Life of Martin Luther.* Nashville: Abingdon Press.

Balfour, Walter. 2019. *An Inquiry into the Scriptural Import of the Words Sheol, Hades, Tartarus, and Gehenna: All Translated Hell, in the Common English Version.* Los Angeles, CA: Hardpress Publishing.

Ball, Scott Blake. 2019. "A Brief History of Mountain Brook Picking on Birmingham." AL.COM. March 7. https://www.al.com/opinion/2016/02/a_brief_history_of_mountain_br.html. Retrieved April 4, 2020.

Barker, Kenneth (General Editor). 1995. *The NIV Study Bible.* Grand Rapids, MI: Zondervan Publishing House.

Bell, Rob. 2012. *Love Wins: A Book about Heaven, Hell, and the Fate of Every Person Who Ever Lived.* New York: HarperOne.

Bhamwiki, 2012. "Jack Trawick." https://www.bhamwiki.com/w/Jack_Trawick. Retrieved, April 5, 2020.

Bonhoeffer, Dietrich. 2003. *Discipleship.* Minneapolis, MN: Fortress Press.

Bonhoeffer, Dietrich. 1995. *Ethics.* New York: Touchstone Books.

Briggs, David. 2019. *Who Worries about Hell the Most.* Christianity Today. https://www.christianitytoday.com/news/2019/february/hell-belief-anxiety-arda-baylor-university.html. Retrieved: 2.17.2020.

Bright, Taylor. 2004. "Is Jack Trawick Still a ... Menace to Society?" *Birmingham Post-Herald*. January 15. http://www.crime-research.org/news/2004/01/Mess1501.html. Retrieved April 4, 2020.

Buckley, William F., Jr. 1986. *God and Man at Yale: The Superstitions of "Academic Freedom."* Washington, D.C.: Regnery Publishing.

Buss, Arnold H. 1975. *A Temperament Theory of Personality Development*. New York: Wiley.

Claiborne, Shane. 2016. *The Irresistible Revolution: Living as an Ordinary Radical*. Grand Rapids, MI: Zondervan.

Claiborne, Shane and Campolo, Tony. 2012. *Red Letter Revolution: What If Jesus Really Meant What He Said?* Nashville, TN: Thomas Nelson.

Cooney, Kevin J., Dudley, William (Bill), Peavy, Tammy L., Pincus, Stephen, Smith Greg, and Slack, James D. 2018. *Christ in Job & Career: Daily Devotions for Christians at Work*. Lexington, KY: Emeth Press.

Cooney, Kevin J., Dudley, William (Bill), Lantz, Jonathan, Meconnahey, Christopher Sean, Peavy, Tammy L., Pincus, Stephen, and Slack, James D. 2017. *The Christ Worker: Devotions for Career and Workplace*. Lexington, KY: Emeth Press.

Court of Criminal Appeals of Alabama. 1995. *Davis v. State*. https://law.justia.com/cases/alabama/court-of-appeals-criminal/1997/cr-93-1364-0.html. Retrieved 6.10.2020.

Court of Criminal Appeals of Alabama. 2006. *Jimmy Davis v. State of Alabama*. https://caselaw.findlaw.com/al-court-of-criminal-appeals/1083183.html. Retrieved 6.10.2020.

de Sade, Marquis. 1795. *Philosophy in the Boudoir*. Reprinted with translation by Joachim Neugroschel and introduction by Francine de Plessix Gray. 2006. New York: Penguin Books.

Dickens, Charles. 2018. A Christmas Carol. Orinda, CA: Sea Wolf Press.

Ehrman, Bart D. 2020. *Heaven and Hell: A History of the Afterlife*. New York: Simon & Schuster.

Executed, 2009. "Jack Harrison Trawick Executed June 11, 2009 06:17 p.m. by Lethal Injection in Alabama." http://www.clarkprosecutor.org/html/death/US/trawick1168.htm. Retrieved April 8, 2020.

Ex parte, 1997. *Trawick, Jack Harrison v. State*. Feb. 28. Supreme Court of Alabama. https://caselaw.findlaw.com/al-supreme-court/1284730.html. Retrieved, April 8, 2020.

Fahmy, Dalia. 2018. *Key Findings About Americans' Belief in God*. Pew Research Center. https://www.pewresearch.org/fact-tank/2018/04/25/key-findings-about-americans-belief-in-god/. Retrieved: 2.17.2020.

Freidenreich, David M. 2017. "Food and Table Fellowship." In Levine, Amy-Jill and Brettler, Marc Zvi (editors). 2017. *The Jewish Annotated*

New Testament. 2nd Edition. Oxford, UK: Oxford University Press. Pp: 650-653.

Genitron.com, 2020. https://www.genitron.com/Handgun/Raven/Pistol/P-25/25-Auto/Variant-1. Retrieved, 7.6.2020.

Hart, David Bentley. 2019. *That All Shall Be Saved: Heaven, Hell, and Universal Salvation.* New Haven, CT: Yale University Press.

Heidegger, Martin. 1968. *What is Called Thinking.* New York: Harper & Row.

Heidegger, Martin. 1962. *Being and Time.* New York: Harper & Row.

Hicks, Stephen R.C. 2011. *Explaining Postmodernism: Skepticism and Socialism from Rousseau to Foucault.* Tempe, AZ: Scholarly Publishing.

Hoeveler, J., Jr. 1996. *The Postmodernist Turn: American Thought and Culture in the 1970s.* Lanham, Maryland: Rowman and Littlefield.

Holly, Michael M. 2020. "Morning Thoughts." *Life Track: Daily.* February 6. Hoover, AL: Bluff Park United Methodist Church.

Husserl, Edmund. 2017. *Ideas: General Introduction to Pure Phenomenology.* London: Routledge.

Ilan, Tal. 2017. "Gender." In Levine, Amy-Jill and Brettler, Marc Zvi (editors). 2017. *The Jewish Annotated New Testament.* 2nd Edition. Oxford, UK: Oxford University Press. Pp. 611-614.

IQ.2020.https://www.verywellmind.com/what-is-a-genius-iq-score-2795585. Retrieved 6.10.2020

Jimmy Davis – Alabama Death Row. 2017. *My Crime Library.* https://mycrimelibrary.com/jimmy-davis-alabama-death-row/. Retrieved 6.10.2020.

Kairos, 2020. Kairos Prison Ministry. https://www.kairosprisonministry.org/. Retrieved 8.20.2020.

Keller, Timothy. 2014. *Prayer: Experiencing Awe and Intimacy with God.* New York: Penguin Books.

Kistemaker, Simon J. 1980. *The Parables: Understand the Stories Jesus Told.* Grand Rapids, MI: Baker Books.

Kraemer, Ross S. 2017. "Jewish Family Life in First Century CE." In Levine, Amy-Jill and Brettler, Marc Zvi (editors). 2017. *The Jewish Annotated New Testament.* 2nd Edition. Oxford, UK: Oxford University Press. Pp 604-608.

Kinnaman, Gary. 1999. *Dumb Things Smart Christians Believe: Misbeliefs that Keep Us from Experiencing God's Grace.* Minneapolis, MN: Bethany House Publishers.

"Letter by Jack Trawick" 2002. *Murder of Aileen Pruitt*. June 11. https://groups.google.com/forum/#!topic/alt.true-crime/1lcdw0pXiJo. Retrieved, April 4, 2020.

Levine, Amy-Jill and Brettler, Marc Zvi (editors). 2017. *The Jewish Annotated New Testament*. 2nd Edition. Oxford, UK: Oxford University Press.

Levine, Amy-Jill. 2014. *Short Stories by Jesus: The Enigmatic Parables of a Controversial Rabbi*. New York: HarperOne.

Macarthur, John. 2015. *Parables: The Mysteries of God's Kingdom Revealed Through the Stories Jesus Told*. New York: Nelson Books.

Machen, J. Gresham. 2013. *Christianity and Liberalism*. Eugene, Oregon: Wipf & Stock.

McWhorter, Diane. 2001. *Carry Me Home: Birmingham, Alabama: The Climactic Battle of the Civil Rights Revolution*. New York: Simon and Schuster Paperbacks.

Morris, Leon. 1999. *The Gospel According to Matthew*. Grand Rapids, MI: William B. Eerd Publishing Co.

Murphy, Carlyle. 2015. *Most Americans Believe in Heaven ... and Hell*. Pew Research Center. https://www.pewresearch.org/fact-tank/2015/11/10/most-americans-believe-in-heaven-and-hell/. Retrieved: 2/17/2020.

NG, Christina. 2011. "The Business of 'Murderability': Websites Selling Murder Memorability. November 7. *ABC News*. https://abcnews.go.com/US/business-murderabilia-websites-selling-murder-memorabilia/story?id=14896607. Retrieved April 4, 2020.

Preach Arizona. 2008. "The Scriptures Where Jesus Speaks on Love." http://www.preacharizona.com/2008/10/scriptures-where-jesus-speaks-on-love.html. Retrieved: 2/17/2020.

Paterson, Martin. Editor. 2015. *The Prisoner's Dilemma (Classical Philosophical Arguments)*. Cambridge, UK: Cambridge University Press.

Radino, John A. 2009. *Lutheran and Catholic Reconciliation on Justification*. Grand Rapids, MI: Wm. B. Eerdmans Publishing Company.

Reeves, Jay. 2003. "Details of Murder Posted on Internet." Associated Press. December 28. https://www.tuscaloosanews.com/article/DA/20031228/News/606119776/TL. Retrieved April 4, 2020.

Roberts, Gary G. (2015). *Developing Christian Servant Leadership: Faith-Based Character Growth at Work*. New York: Palgrave Macmillan.

Shakespeare, William. 2013. *The Tragedy of Macbeth*. New York: Simon and Schuster. (Act 2, Scene 2).

Shelton, W. Brian. 2014. *Prevenient Grace: God's Provision for Fallen Humanity*. Anderson, IN: Francis Asbury Press.

Simmons, Bryan. 2019. *Ninety-Five Reflections: Martin Luther's 95 Theses Yesterday and Today*. Ames, IA: PB & Company.

Slack, James D. 2017. *Abortion, Execution, and the Consequences of Taking Life*. Routledge Taylor & Francis. 2nd Edition. Kindle Edition.

Slack, James D. 2014, 2011, 2009. *Abortion, Execution, and the Consequences of Taking Life*. New Brunswick, N.J.: Transaction Publishers.

Slack, James D., Meconnahey, Christopher Sean, and Dudley, William (Bill). 2015. *Devotions for the Christian Public Servant*. Lexington, KY: Emeth Press.

Smith, Sam A. 2013. *The Olivet Discourse: A Reconstruction of the Text from Matthew, Mark, and Luke, with Commentary*. Raleigh, NC: Biblical Reader Communication.

Steigmann-Gall, Richard. 2003. *The Holy Reich: Nazi Conceptions of Christianity*. Cambridge, UK: Cambridge University Press.

Strong, James. 2010. *Strong's Concordance with Hebrew & Greek Lexicon*. Peabody, MA: Hendrickson Publishers. http://www.eliyah.com/lexicon.html. Retrieved: 2.17.2020.

Supreme Court of Alabama. 1998. *Ex Parte Davis* https://law.justia.com/cases/alabama/supreme-court/1998/1961441-1.html.

Trimm, Tobias. 2019. *Richard Rorty and the Problem of Post Modern Experience: A Reconstruction*. Lenham, MA: Lexington Books.

Turner, David L. 2008. *Matthew*. Grand Rapids, MI: Baker Academics.

Upper Room – Emmaus, 2020. https://support.upperroom.org/en/support/solutions/folders/19000003298#:~:text=The%20Walk%20to%20Emmaus%C2%AE%20is%20grounded%20theologically%20and,Church...%20Wed%2C%2017%20Jul%2C%202019%20at%201-0%3A17%20AM. Retrieved, 8.20.2020.

U.S. Census. 2020. https://www.census.gov/quickfacts/fact/table/annistoncityalabama,AL/PST045219. Retrieved, 6.10.2020

Valleys of Jerusalem. 2020. http://www.land-of-the-bible.com/The_Valleys_of_Jerusalem. Retrieved: 2.20.2020.

Vanhooser, Keven J. 1998. *Is There Meaning in This Text: The Bible, The Reader, and the Morality of Literary Knowledge*. Grand Rapids, MI: Zondervan.

Webb, Stephen H. 2011. "Silence, Noise, and the Voice of Jesus Christ." Perry Aaron (Editor). *Developing Ears to Hear*. Lexington, KY: Emeth Press.

West, Ty. 2015. "Just How Wealthy is Mountain Brook Compared to the Rest of the Nation's Most Affluent Places?" *Birmingham Business Journal*. November 30. https://www.bizjournals.com/birmingham/

news/2015/11/30/just-how-wealthy-is-mountain-brook-compared-to-the.html#g/286912/1. Retrieved April 4, 2020.

Whalan, Matthew Vernon. 2013. *The Little Book of Freedom.* Troy, New York: The Troy Book Makers.

Woods, Tim. 1999. *Beginning of Postmodernism.* Manchester, UK: Manchester University Press.

Index

agape love
   defined, 2, 3, 12; Jack Trawick, 37-43; James D. Slack, 98; Jimmy Davis, Jr., 59-65, 71; justice of Jesus' love, 98
Anniston, Alabama,
   description, 48; in comparison, 104; Jimmy Davis, Jr., 49-51, 54, 61, 70
"Anthony," xvii, 91-94, 99

Bonhoeffer, Dietrich
   truth, xvi, postmodernism, 4
borderline intellectual disability
   defined, 61; Jimmy Davis, Jr., 61, 107
Buckley, William F
   postmodernism, 4, 5, 8

Calvin, John, 66
   prayer, 66
Campolo, Tony, 10
capital crimes against Christ
   defined, 19; discussed, xiii, xv, xvi; James D. Slack, 90-96, 99; Matthew 25, 102; murder's noise, 101; the reader, 106; standing the left of Christ, 96
Claiborne, Shane, 6, 10
comfort zone, spiritual, 2, 4, 6

domesticated, 10, 11; God's Hand, 87, 88, 90, 97, 107, 108; Jack Trawick, 43; lost, 90, 106; playground, 78, 79, 99; the goats to His left, 96
disobedience to God, 19, 75, 94, 102, 105; capital crime xiii, 79, 107; childish disobedience, 85, 99; in sufficient obedience, 96
domestication of God's expectations, xv, xvi, 7, 10, 11, 43, 97, 98, 106, 107
Donaldson Correctional Facility, 55, 86, 88, 89

Emmaus Movement, 58, 84, 86
execution junky, 92, 94
execution team
   agape love, 37, 38, 40, 43, 94; Jack Trawick's anger, 34

faith-alone vs. faith-plus-deeds, xvii-xix
Finney, Charles Grandison, 79, 80, 99, 104

Gach, Stephanie Alexis, 28-30, 33, 36

Hart, David Bentley, 8
Hazel, Johnny, 51-54, 57, 69, 71, 73
Heaven
   afterlife option, xiv; dead to, 102; faith-alone vs. faith-plus-deeds, xvii, xviii;
   forgiveness, 40; Jesus, xviii, 4, 6, 8, 9, 42, 70, 103; lesson, 14; speculation about, xv
hell
   afterlife option, xiv; avoiding, xiii, 12-14, 16, 22, 23, 46, 69, 76, 106; belief in, 3, 4, 7, 10; choice, 43; churches, 10; forgotten, 1, 6; gift

still wrapped, 75; Gehenna Valley as metaphor, 17, 43; Jesus. xviii, 2-4, 8, 10; location, 17; process, 21, 43, 44; situation, 2; state of mind, 45, 47, 73

Holman Correctional Facility background, xiii, xvii, 19, 24, 37, 42, 54, 55; death row, 55, 58-60, 66, 69, 73. 88,89, 91, 92, 95, 99

Ilan, Tal, 17

justice of Jesus love, 100, 102, 103; as the core of the Jesus-Means-Business paradigm, 98

Kairos Prison Ministry, 58-68, 86-89; Pony's brownies/Michael's story, 102

Levine, Amy-Jill, 6, 8, 11
Luther, Martin, xvii

Macbeth
and book title, xiv; innocent's sleep, xiv; murder's noise, 101
Machen, J. Gresham, 15
Manson, Charles, 22, 27, 43
Mountain Brook, Alabama comparison, 104; description 24; Jack Trawick, 24, 25
Morris, Leon 18

Oberlin (village and College), 79
Olivet Discourse, 15

parable
contemporary: A Gift Still Wrapped, 77, 94, 96, Dark Letter, 22, 23, 27; Lost Ears, 1, 2, Murder's Noise, 101, The Barred Door, 47, 56; and the Holy Spirit, 18, 19; definition, 12;

Jesus: as the good professor, 16, 17, doing the afflicting, 8, Jewishness, 16, use of parables, xviii; Jewish metaphors in Jesus' parables, 17; Parables in Matthew 25: analysis, 102, 103, capital crimes against Christ, xiii, xix, 19, 90, 102, overview, 12-16; Parable of Talents: capital crimes against Christ, 19, expectation, 46, 69, 70, Illustration 3.1, 45, Jesus escalation of punishment, 103, overview, 13, 14, moral lesson, 46, talent defined, 46; Parable of the Sheep and the Goats: capital crimes against Christ, 19, expectation, 76, Illustration 4.1, 75, 76, Jesus highest escalation of punishment, 103, Jewish tradition, 76, overview, 14-16, moral lesson, 76; Parable of the Ten Virgins: capital crimes against Christ, 19, expectation, 22, Illustration 2.1, 21, moral lesson, 22, overview, 12, 13, 102, 103.

paradigm
defined, 4; Jesus-Loves-Me Paradigm: defined, 4, grandmother and aunt, 82, 96, and Jesus-Means-Business Paradigm, 103, 106, Jimmy Davis, Jr., 69, 71, justice of His love, 98, 106, knowing Jesus, 40, postmodernism, 4-8, prison ministry, 91, scripture, 9; Jesus-Means-Business Parable: defined, 4, hell, 8,9, 40, Jack Trawick, 43, James D. Slack, 82,83, 98, and Jesus-Loves-Me Paradigm, 103, 106, Jimmy Davis, Jr., 69, 71, justice of His love, 98

postmodernism
and the least of His, 97; consequences, 5-8; definition, 4; du-

plicity, 10, 11; domesticating God's calling, 78; emergence, 4, 5; Murder's Noise, 102-106
Pruitt, Frances Aileen, 27-29, 30

Richards, Betty Jo, 27, 29, 42
Roberts, Gary, 2

South Amherst, Ohio
comparison, 104, 105; description, 79; James D. Slack, 79-83
Spears, Britney, 27, 30, 32
spiritscape, xv, 102, 107; definition, 101
Susan, 95, 96, 105

Topeth, in Gehenna Valley, 17
The Christian Public Servant, 11; James D. Slack, 85; and Jimmy Davis, Jr., 67, 68
Turner, David L., 18

Victims of Crime & Leniency (VOCAL), 91

Z-number/status, 55

www.ingramcontent.com/pod-product-compliance
Lightning Source LLC
Chambersburg PA
CBHW050832160426
43192CB00010B/2001